Neil 1996

Perfect
Step By Step Cooking

Produced by Copyright Studio, Paris
Editor: Jean-Paul Paireault
Cookery Editor: Catherine Monnet
Art Director: Jacques Hennaux
Design: Sandrine Desbordes

CLB 2373
This edtion published in 1993 by Coombe Books
© 1990 CLB Publishing
Printed and bound in Hong Kong by Leefung Asco Printers Ltd.
All rights reserved.
ISBN 0 86283 790 1

Perfect
Step By Step Cooking

COOMBE BOOKS

CONTENTS

INTRODUCTION

The title of this cookery book gives more than just a clue as to its contents, but it still tells only half the story. The recipes included here are indeed all about the style and art of modern cooking, but they are not about complicated preparation or cooking techniques. Just the opposite. These recipes are about helping you to produce, simply and without fuss, in your own kitchen, the type of dishes seen in today's more fashionable restaurants. Dishes which, with their emphasis on increasingly artful and elegant presentation, often look dauntingly difficult to reproduce.

This book, however, enables you to do just that by presenting each recipe with explicit instructions in an illustrated, step-by-step format, including, wherever it might be useful, specific preparation techniques. The necessary ingredients and utensils are carefully listed at the beginning of each recipe and, to stimulate your taste buds, the recipes are preceded by a beautiful colour photograph of the finished dish, together with a detailed description of the dish itself. Furthermore, each recipe has been tested and retested by its originator, French chef Frédéric Lebain, to make it as easy as possible for you to obtain the same perfect results as he has.

The recipes have, of course, been developed with the everyday cook in mind, but occasionally they include special ingredients which may be more difficult to find. In this case, alternative ingredients are always suggested.

So, whether it's simply for a family meal or for an elegant dinner party, bring a little restaurant glamour into your home with Perfect Cooking.

BASIL

Fresh basil is one of the best herbs to add to tomato or egg dishes. The leaves, can also be used whole in green salads, or chopped and added to a vinaigrette. Use it to flavour butter or with bland fish.

ROSEMARY

Rosemary is traditionally used with lamb, but also goes well with halibut and can even be used in salads or in cheese dishes. Use either whole sprigs of the herb or just the spiky leaves.

THE HERBS

Fresh herbs not only add flavour to but improve the appearance of any gourmet dish. Certain herbs marry well with particular foods but there are no hard and fast rules. A keen cook can experiment to create original and tasty combinations.

THYME

Thyme is best known as an ingredient of bouquets garnis. It has a strong flavour and should be added sparingly to grilled meat or fish. Chop the fresh leaves, and add to mashed potatoes or other vegetable dishes.

DILL

Dill is particularly good in fish dishes. Try adding the chopped leaves to green or raw vegetable salads. The seeds are good with cucumber, or crushed in lamb stews.

CHERVIL

Similar to parsley in appearance, it can be used in the same ways, too, although its slightly aniseed flavour means it should be used more sparingly.

PARSLEY

Curly-leaved parsley is best
reserved for decoration ; use the
flat-leaved variety for cooking.
The leaves can be used whole,
or chopped and added to salads
and sauces or sprinkled over
cooked vegetables.

CHIVES

Chives have a mild onion flavour which makes them
a versatile seasoning for many dishes, particularly in soups,
with freshwater fish and in sauces such as
Béarnaise or vinaigrette.

CORIANDER

Coriander is an annual plant native to the Mediterranean
region but which now grows wild in most parts of Europe.It
is one of the oldest herbs known to man and the leaves can
be used in a variety of dishes from salads to curries.

BAY

An evergreen shrub, native to Mediterranean
countries,whose leaves can be used fresh, or
dried, sliced, chopped or powdered
to add flavour to stocks, stews and pâtés.
Indispensable in bouquets garnis.

MINT

The mint plant comes originally
from the Mediterranean, where it
was highly esteemed in ancient
times as a symbol of hospitality. Its
uses are wide ranging.

SAGE

Sage is used not only in sage and onion
stuffing, but also with roast pork or in
beef stews. The fresh leaves, chopped, are
good in salads and on tomatoes.

TARRAGON

Tarragon has a distinctive flavour; it can be
finely chopped and added to a vinaigrette.
It also enhances meat, fish and chicken
dishes. Chopped and added to butter it
flavours bland vegetables.

LEMON GRASS

Lemon grass is a member of the mint family.
The leaves have a strong, lemony scent and can be
used to season a variety of savoury dishes.

JUNIPER BERRIES
Juniper berries have a peppery, slightly resinous flavour. They are best lightly crushed and added to game dishes and marinade for raw fish.

CUMIN
An aromatic plant, the seeds are dried and used crushed or whole in soups and breads, and to flavour meat and fish dishes.

THE SPICES

Spices can transform an ordinary meal into an adventure. Ready-ground spices rapidly lose their flavour, so buy only small quantities at a time, store in airtight containers and never keep them for more than a year.

NUTMEG
Although usually sold ground, nutmeg is best bought as white kernels and freshly grated, as required. It is commonly used in any type of potato dish, or in white sauces and soufflés.

CLOVES
Cloves are the dried, unopened buds of and evergreen tree. They give a sharp, spicy flavour when added whole to stews or marinades. When finely ground, they are often used in association with cinnamon for desserts.

CURRY POWDER
This is a mixture of ground Asian spices, most commonly turmeric, coriander, chilli, cumin, mustard seed and fenugreek. The different proportions of these spices accounts for the degree of hotness of the curry powder.

CAYENNE PEPPER
The dried pods of a red chilli pepper native to Central America are ground to produce this hot spice.

CARDAMOM
Cardamom is a member of the ginger family, native to India and also extensively cultivated in Malabar and Ceylon. Use the seeds to flavour hot fruit punches, pickles, mulled wines, breads, biscuits and desserts.

TURMERIC
This tropical Asian spice is always sold ground. The bitter powder is used in oriental cuisine to colour rice dishes. It is also a common ingredient in curry powders.

CINNAMON
Cinnamon is in fact dried bark which rolls up on drying to form "quills". It is mostly used in puddings, sweet sauces and ice cream, but is becoming more popular in fish and meat dishes.

CORIANDER
Coriander seeds can be used either ground or whole and are must common in sausages, pickles, puddings, Danish pastries and cakes.

VANILLA
The cured pod of a climbing orchid native to Central America, vanilla is used to flavour sweet sauces, cakes, chocolate and puddings.

MIXED HERBS
Ready prepared mixed dried herbs, usually consisting of thyme, marjoram, parsley, rosemary and basil. They can be used in most any savoury dish.

PINK PEPPERCORNS
Cultivated in the Bourbon Islands, these peppercorns or berries have both a sweet and savoury taste.

PAPRIKA
Paprika is a mild spice ground from sweet peppers. It lends a slightly spicy, hot flavour to stews (Hungarian Goulash, notably), and can also be used in sauces for red meats. Try a pinch in a white sauce to enliven the flavour.

FIVE-SPICE POWDER
Made with equal parts of ground brown peppercorns, cinnamon, cloves, fennel and star anise, five-spice powder is most frequently used in Chinese cooking.

SMALL CARVING KNIFE
Equipped with a long fine, blade
for thin slicing.

NON-STICK, SAUCEPAN
Ideal for cooking
medium quantities, such as
pastas and sauces.

THE UTENSILS

A cook's utensils, like a workman's tools, can often

determine his success or failure. Well constructed pots

and pans, sharp knives and proper cooking tools, greathy

facilitate food preparation. Today we have the added

advantage of time saving machines, mixers,

processors, etc.

PASTA MACHINE
Enables you to make fresh homemade pasta.
It usually consists of a roller for flattening the dough
and an attachment for cutting pasta in to various
shapes : tagliatelle, spaghetti, etc.

GRATER
For cutting or grating
different shapes of vegetables quickly
and evenly, such as julienne slices, etc.

MEDIUM CHOPPING KNIFE
A medium-sized knife, good for chopping vegetables and
small cuts of meat. It is also used to remove the flesh from
tomatoes or to peel fruits such as lemons.

FINE SIEVE
To strain sauces and
purées, to eliminate
impurities. It is often
lined with fine muslin
for straining stocks or
liquid sauces.

VEGETABLE PEELER
Ideal for peeling most
fruits and vegetables ;
also used to remove
fish bones.

GLASS BAKING DISH
Recommended for baking, especially for
browning, as in "au gratin" dishes or spare
ribs. Very resistant to high temperatures.

RUBBER SPATULA
Ideal for transferring creams and sauces from one
container to another without waste.

LARGE NON-STICK FLAMEPROOF CASSEROLE
Used for cooking large joints of meat
or vegetables. It can also be used to sauté or
prepare dishes that require long,
slow cooking.

HEAVY-BOTTOMED SAUCEPAN
Used for bringing liquids such as milk
to a rapid boil, or for making small
quantities of sauce.

FILLETING KNIFE
Quite flexible, used mostly for
filleting any variety of fish.

LARGE NON-STICK FRYING PAN
For cooking large quantities of rice,
seafood or anything else in bulk.

LADLE
For spooning up liquids
or creams. Can be used
as a measure ; the
quantities vary with the
different models.

CLEAVER
Used for breaking up or chopping bones
or for flattening meat into scallops.

HAND-HELD ELECTRIC MIXER
Indispensable for liquidising sauces, it has
various speeds and can be battery operated
for convenience. It is equally useful for
making fresh fruit purées or "coulis".

MIXING BOWL
With its slightly rounded base,
this is excellent for preparing
pastry dough, for making sweet
or savoury sauces and also for
whipping cream or egg whites.

LARGE CHOPPING KNIFE
For finely chopping herbs or
vegetables, or for cutting vegetables
into various shapes.

METAL WHISK
Used in the preparation of numerous mixtures,
sauces, creams, etc. The large wire whisk is
used to beat double cream or egg whites.

ALL-PURPOSE KNIFE
Enables you to trim
and shape vegetables or for
any basic cutting job. Also
used for boning chicken.

CONSOMMÉ

WITH

CRUNCHY

VEGETABLES

SERVES : 6

PREPARATION TIME : 45 Minutes
COOKING TIME : 2 Hours 30 Minutes

*A clear, light soup of enriched meat stock, which
can be served either hot or cold. Raw, diced
vegetables are added at the last minute to retain
their crispness and fresh flavour.*

INGREDIENTS

- ☐ 1kg/2¼lbs stewing beef (have the butcher chop the bones)
- ☐ 3 carrots
- ☐ 2 turnips
- ☐ 200g/8oz potatoes
- ☐ 100g/4oz French beans
- ☐ ½ large celeriac
- ☐ 1 leek
- ☐ Bouquet garni (parsley, thyme, bay leaf)
- ☐ 100g/4oz peas
- ☐ 2 egg whites
- ☐ 2 tbsps soy sauce
- ☐ 2 sprigs parsley
- ☐ Salt and pepper

1 Cut off any fat on the meat; roll it up and tie neatly. Reserve the bones.

2 Peel the carrots and turnip (reserve the peelings). Cut in slices, then stick and finally dice.

3 Make the bouquet garni by tying together the parsley, thyme and bay leaf.

4 In a casserole, cover the meat, bones and vegetable peelings and add the bouquet garni with cold water. Cook for 2 hours 30 minutes, skimming off the foam.

5 Peel the potatoes and cube them, along with the French beans. Put the potatoes in water to prevent discoloration and set aside.

6 Peel, trim and cube the celeriac. Wash and finely dice the leek. Shell the peas.

7 Boil the diced vegetables separately, then the peas. Drain, rinse and set aside.

8 When the meat is done, remove, slice through the string and cube half of the meat (reserve the other half for another use). Allow the stock and meat to cool.

9 Lightly beat (5 seconds) the egg whites into the leeks, add to the cooled consommé. Bring to a boil, and simmer for 5 minutes, stirring constantly. Add the soy sauce and pepper.

10 Strain the stock through a sieve lined with muslin. Keep the stock warm.

11 Wash and trim the parsley. Dry well and finely chop all the leafy parts.

12 Distribute the vegetables and meat between 6 soup plates, pour over the hot consommé, and serve with chopped parsley.

TURNIP

AND

CABBAGE SOUP

SERVES : 6

PREPARATION TIME : 30 Minutes
COOKING TIME : 1 Hour 20 Minutes

*This recipe is a modernized version of a basic
country soup, which once served as a complete
meal, containing meat, vegetables and bread.
The ingredients are simple to find year-round
and inexpensive.*

INGREDIENTS

☐ 200g/8oz smoked bacon
☐ ½ cabbage
☐ 800g/2lbs turnips
☐ 1 onion
☐ 3 tbsps olive oil
☐ Bouquet garni (parsley, thyme, bay leaf)
☐ 10 black olives
☐ 1 French stick
☐ 200ml/8 fl oz double cream
☐ 6 sprigs chervil, chopped
☐ Salt and pepper

1 Cut off and reserve the rind of the bacon. Slice into thin strips, then dice.

2 Place the bacon in a saucepan of cold water to cover, and bring to a boil. Rinse and drain in a sieve. Set aside.

3 Remove the outer leaves of the cabbage and slice thinly.

4 Blanch the cabbage strips for 4 minutes in boiling salted water. Rinse and drain in a sieve.

5 With a small knife, peel the turnips. Cut in two, then into smaller pieces.

6 Peel the onion, cut in two then chop finely.

7 Fry the onion in 2 tbsps hot oil. Add the bacon rind and the turnips. Cook, shaking often, for 5 minutes.

8 Add water or stock (approximately 1½ litres/3 pints), the bouquet garni, salt and pepper. Cook, covered, over a moderate heat for 45 minutes.

9 Stone the olives and chop finely.

10 Remove the bacon from the soup and discard. Blend the soup smooth. Add the cabbage, and cook, stirring often, for 15 minutes over a low heat.

11 Slice the bread, and toast lightly. Brush with the remaining olive oil. Place in the oven for 1 minute.

12 Stir in the cream, smoked bacon pieces and chopped olives. Heat through and serve with the toasts. Sprinkle the soup with the chopped fresh chervil.

COLD MUSSEL SOUP

WITH

SAFFRON

SERVES : 6

PREPARATION TIME : 45 Minutes
COOKING TIME : 10 Minutes
CHILLING : 2 Hours

This is an elegant seafood soup perfect for warm summer evenings. Mussels and saffron are complementary flavours, and the use of real saffron threads is important. Crisp garlic croutons garnished with lumpfish roe complete the dish.

INGREDIENTS

- ☐ 1 litre/2 pints mussels
- ☐ 2 shallots, finely chopped
- ☐ ¼ litre/½ pint white wine
- ☐ ½ cucumber
- ☐ ½ litre/1 pint fish stock
- ☐ ¼ litre/½ pint double cream
- ☐ 1 pinch saffron powder
- ☐ 6 slices French bread
- ☐ 1 clove garlic (central shoot removed)
- ☐ 1 jar lumpfish roe
- ☐ 1½ tbsps chives, chopped
- ☐ Saffron fronds
- ☐ Salt and pepper

1 Scrape and remove the cords from the mussels. Soak and wash them well. Ensure that the mussels are clean before going on to the next step.

2 Place the mussels in a large frying pan, add the shallots, pepper and white wine. Cook covered for 7 minutes.

3 Once the mussels are open and cool, remove from the shells.

4 Strain the cooking juices through a sieve lined with a piece of muslin. Discard the sand and impurities.

5 Peel the cucumber lengthwise with a vegetable peeler.

6 Cut the cucumber into chunks. Remove bands of flesh, working down to the centre and seeds. Cut the flesh into a fine julienne.

7 In a casserole, bring the stock, cooking juices, cream, saffron to a boil.

8 Once the soup is boiling, season with salt and pepper, remove it from the heat and blend until smooth. Allow to cool slightly, then refrigerate for 2 hours.

9 Toast the slices of bread evenly on each side.

10 Remove the central shoot of the garlic. Rub the garlic over the toasts, and spoon some lumpfish roe over each slice.

11 Chop the chives.

12 Arrange all the ingredients together decoratively to present the soup. Sprinkle the saffron fronds over the soup just before serving.

CRAB SALAD

IN

ORANGE SHELLS

SERVES : 6

PREPARATION TIME : 35 Minutes

This crab salad is attractively served in hollowed-out orange shells for an original presentation. The addition of the orange flesh gives a contrasting sweet and acid taste to the seafood and vegetables. Imitation crab meat can be used, if desired.

INGREDIENTS

☐ 3 large oranges (or 6 small)
☐ 1 avocado pear
☐ Juice of 1 lemon
☐ 1 egg yolk
☐ 1 tsp mustard
☐ 200ml/8 fl oz oil
☐ 1 tbsp tomato ketchup
☐ 1 tsp Cognac
☐ Few drops Tabasco
☐ 1 tsp Worcestershire sauce
☐ ½ onion
☐ 100g/4oz small prawns
☐ 10 (300g/12oz) crab sticks, fresh
   or imitation
☐ 2 tomatoes
☐ ½ bunch chervil
☐ Salt and pepper

1 Halve the oranges and remove the flesh without crushing it. Reserve the shells for presentation.

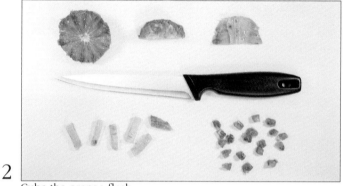

2 Cube the orange flesh.

3 Halve the avocado. Remove the stone, and peel. Dice, and coat with lemon juice to prevent discoloration.

4 Mix together the mustard, egg yolk, salt and pepper. Gradually whisk in the oil to make a mayonnaise.

5

When thick, add the ketchup, Cognac, Tabasco and Worcestershire sauce. Blend thoroughly.

9

Remove the stalks from the tomatoes. Plunge in boiling water for 10 seconds to facilitate peeling.

6

Peel and halve the onion. Chop one half finely.

10

Then plunge the tomatoes in cold water, peel off the skin, and cube the flesh. Discard the juice and seeds. Reserve 2 tbsps for decoration.

7

Peel the prawns. Set aside the meat.

11

Mix all the ingredients into the mayonnaise, and check for seasoning.

8

Cut the crab sticks in half then shred. Set aside.

12

Fill each orange shell with the salad, and garnish with the reserved tomato and chervil.

SPINACH SALAD

WITH

CHICKEN LIVERS

AND SWEETBREADS

SERVES : 6

PREPARATION TIME : 30 Minutes
COOKING TIME : 15 Minutes

*A wonderfully healthy salad, rich in iron, that
is easy to prepare and elegant to serve. The
original sauce is a mayonnaise base thinned
with stock and flavoured with aromatic herbs.*

INGREDIENTS

- ☐ 1 curly endive
- ☐ 2 small heads radicchio lettuce
- ☐ 200g/8oz fresh spinach
- ☐ 300g/12oz lamb sweetbreads
- ☐ 1 sprig thyme
- ☐ 1 bay leaf
- ☐ 200g/8oz chicken livers
- ☐ 1 egg yolk
- ☐ 1 tbsp mustard
- ☐ 250ml/10 fl oz oil
- ☐ 3 tbsps fresh, chopped herbs (chives, tarragon, chervil)
- ☐ 1 carrot
- ☐ 1 tomato
- ☐ 50ml/2 fl oz chicken stock
- ☐ 1 tbsp vinegar
- ☐ 2 tbsps butter
- ☐ Salt and pepper

1 Wash and trim the curly endive, spinach and radicchio. Slice the spinach into wide strips.

2 Blanch the sweetbreads in a flameproof casserole of salted water with the thyme and bay leaf. Bring to a boil and cook for 6 minutes. Remove and rinse.

3 Pull or cut the skin off the sweetbreads. Cut them into small pieces. Gently remove the nerve of the chicken livers.

4 Make a mayonnaise by mixing together the egg yolk, mustard, salt and pepper. Gradually whisk in 200ml/8 fl oz of the oil.

5 When the mayonnaise has thickened, stir in 2 tbsps of chopped herbs (chives, tarragon, chervil). Mix well and set aside.

6 Peel and slice the carrots thinly. Julienne the slices.

7 Carve around the heart of the tomato to remove only the flesh. Cut the flesh into strips, then cube.

8 Add the stock to the mayonnaise drop by drop, mixing in well, then stir in 1 tbsp of vinegar and the tomato cubes.

9 In a large frying pan, heat the remaining oil and the butter; when bubbling, sear the livers, then the sweetbreads.

10 Shaking the pan continuously, continue to cook the livers and sweetbreads for 5 to 10 minutes. Season with salt and pepper and 1 tbsp of herbs. Set aside.

11 Toss the spinach, curly endive and radicchio lettuce in a little of the mayonnaise. Serve the remaining mayonnaise in a small bowl.

12 Spread a bed of salad on each plate, sprinkle over the carrot, and top with the livers and sweetbreads. Sprinkle with the remaining chopped herbs.

JELLIED CHICKEN TERRINE WITH VEGETABLE VINAIGRETTE

SERVES : 6

PREPARATION TIME : 35 Minutes
COOKING TIME : 1 Hour 15 Minutes
COOLING and CHILLING TIME : 10 Hours

A good entrée for entertaining, this is pretty to serve and can be prepared in advance. The terrine, based on chicken stock, contains diced vegetables and boned chicken. It's perfect for those counting their calories.

INGREDIENTS

- [ ] 3 carrots
- [ ] 2 courgettes
- [ ] 100g/4oz French beans, trimmed
- [ ] 100g/4oz peas, shelled
- [ ] 4 tbsps olive oil
- [ ] ½ onion, finely chopped
- [ ] 4 chicken legs
- [ ] 4 chicken livers
- [ ] Thyme
- [ ] Bay leaf
- [ ] 1 egg white, lightly beaten (5 seconds)
- [ ] 1½ sachets gelatine
- [ ] 1 tbsp wine vinegar
- [ ] 1 tsp coriander seeds, crushed
- [ ] Small bunch chives, chopped
- [ ] Small bunch chervil, chopped
- [ ] Salt and pepper

1 Cut the vegetables into sticks. Boil the vegetables individually in salted water, carrots (6 mins), courgettes (3 mins), French beans (8 mins), peas (10 mins). Refresh and drain.

2 Sauté in 1 tbsp oil the onion, carrot trimmings, chicken meat, chicken livers, thyme, bay leaf; cover with water and cook for 35 minutes. Strain the stock through a sieve.

3 Pour the warm stock onto the egg white and mix well. Stir and bring to a boil in a saucepan. Cook for 10 minutes, then strain through a muslin-lined sieve.

4 Soften the gelatine in a little water, and stir into ½ litre/1 pint hot stock. Season and allow to cool for 30 minutes.

5 Pull the chicken meat off the bone and chop finely. Chop the skin finely.

6 Fill the base of your mould or terrine with a layer of the stock, and leave in the refrigerator until firm.

7 Distribute a layer of cut vegetables over the jellied stock. Add a layer of stock, then a layer of meat. Allow to set in the refrigerator.

8 Reserve 3 tbsp of the vegetables and dice. Layer the remaining vegetables, the chicken livers and another layer of stock into the terrine. Chill until firm.

9 Make a vinaigrette by mixing together the vinegar, salt, pepper, crushed coriander, chives and 3 tbsps olive oil. Set aside.

10 Mix the reserved vegetables into the vinaigrette. Adjust seasoning. Set aside.

11 When the terrine has set (8 to 10 hours), dip the base of the mould in hot water for 30 seconds and unmould. Cut into thin slices.

12 Serve garnished with the fresh chervil and the vegetable vinaigrette.

PRAWN SALAD

WITH

BACON

SERVES : 6

PREPARATION TIME : 40 Minutes
COOKING TIME : 25 Minutes

*An attractive first course or a good luncheon
dish if the quantities are increased. The
vinaigrette sauce is quite unique, flavoured
with a reduction of prawn shells cooked in olive
oil.*

INGREDIENTS

- [ ] 36 medium prawns
- [ ] 1 carrot
- [ ] ½ onion
- [ ] ¼ leek
- [ ] 3 tbsps olive oil
- [ ] 100g/4oz lamb's lettuce
- [ ] 1 head fancy lettuce
- [ ] 4 slices bread
- [ ] 1 clove garlic (central shoot removed)
- [ ] 150g/6oz bacon, finely sliced
- [ ] ½ cucumber
- [ ] 1 tbsp wine vinegar
- [ ] ½ bunch chives
- [ ] 1½ tbsps butter
- [ ] Fresh herbs (chives)
- [ ] Salt and pepper

1 Peel the prawns, and remove the heads and tails (reserve). Devein.

2 Peel and roughly chop the carrot, leek and onion.

3 Fry the vegetables with the prawn trimmings and half the peelings in 1 tbsp of oil. Pour in ¼ litre ½ pint water, and cook over a moderate heat for 10 to 15 minutes.

4 Trim, and wash the lamb's lettuce and the inner leaves of the fancy lettuce.

5 Trim the crusts off the bread. Cut into cubes.

6 Halve the garlic, and gently heat in 1 tbsp of oil. Add the bread cubes, and sauté to make croutons. When the bread cubes are golden brown, drain on kitchen paper.

7 Layer the bacon slices and cut them into small, neat strips.

8 Halve the cucumber lengthwise. Peel and remove the seeds with a small spoon. Slice the flesh and then dice.

9 Strain the prawn stock through a fine sieve lined with muslin. Measure out 100ml/4 fl oz.

10 When the stock is cool, whisk in 1 tbsp oil, the vinegar, salt and pepper to taste, and the chopped chives. Set aside.

11 Sauté the prawns and bacon in the butter for 2 minutes. Add a little pepper. Set aside.

12 Serve the mixed salad topped with the prawns, bacon and croutons. Sprinkle over the cucumber and dress with the vinaigrette. Garnish with fresh, chopped herbs.

ROQUEFORT TIMBALES

WITH

FRESH FIGS

SERVES : 6

PREPARATION TIME : 30 Minutes
COOKING TIME : 40 Minutes

*Here is a most original flavour combination
which is absolutely delicious. These cheese-
flavoured egg and cream timbales can be served
to begin the meal, or as a cheese and fruit
course after the main dish.*

INGREDIENTS

- ☐ 150g/6oz Roquefort cheese (or blue cheese)
- ☐ ½ litre/1 pint milk
- ☐ Nutmeg
- ☐ 4 eggs
- ☐ 2 tsps butter
- ☐ 10 fresh figs
- ☐ 6 servings fancy lettuce
- ☐ ½ bunch chives
- ☐ 20 hazelnuts
- ☐ 1 tomato
- ☐ 1 shallot
- ☐ 1 tbsp vinegar
- ☐ 3 tbsps oil
- ☐ Salt and pepper

1 Roughly chop the cheese or crumble with a fork.

2 Bring the milk to a boil with a little salt, pepper and grated nutmeg.

3 Beat the eggs. Whisk the hot milk into the eggs.

4 Add the cheese to the milk and eggs and stir well.

5 Grease 6 ramekins with the butter, then fill almost to the top with the milk and egg mixture.

6 Bake the timbales in a tray of water in a moderate oven (180°C/350°F/Gas Mark 4) for 35 minutes.

7 Trim the stems of the figs, slice, then cube.

8 Wash the lettuce and trim. Dry it well. Chop the chives.

9 Shell the hazelnuts, scrape off the inner skin, and chop finely.

10 Peel the tomato, and chop only the outer flesh. Finely chop the shallot.

11 Make a vinaigrette by whisking together the salt, vinegar, pepper, chives, shallot, hazelnuts and oil.

12 When the timbales are cooked, run a knife around the inside edges of the ramekins, and turn out. Serve on a bed of lettuce, dotted with the figs, and dressed with the vinaigrette.

CREPES FILLED

WITH

VEGETABLES

SERVES : 6

PREPARATION TIME : 1 Hour
COOKING TIME : 50 Minutes
RESTING TIME : 35 Minutes

*A completely vegetarian dish which can be
served as a first course or, in larger quantities,
as a main dish. Delicate buckwheat crepes are
filled with steamed diced vegetables. The rich
chive-butter sauce can be served sparingly on
the side for those watching their diet.*

INGREDIENTS

- ☐ 250g/10oz buckwheat flour
- ☐ 2 eggs
- ☐ 600ml/24 fl oz milk
- ☐ 40g/1¹/₂oz butter, melted
- ☐ 2 carrots
- ☐ 2 medium courgettes
- ☐ 500g/1lb 2oz fresh broad beans
- ☐ 250g/9oz fresh peas
- ☐ 100g/4oz bean sprouts
- ☐ 100g/4oz tinned corn
- ☐ 2 tbsps oil
- ☐ ¹/₂ egg, beaten
- ☐ 3 shallots, chopped
- ☐ 100ml/4 fl oz white wine
- ☐ 150g/6oz butter
- ☐ Small bunch chives, chopped
- ☐ ¹/₂ lemon
- ☐ Fresh herbs (chervil)
- ☐ Salt and pepper

1 Prepare the pancake batter by beating together the buckwheat flour, 1 tsp salt and the eggs. Gradually mix in the milk.

2 Add half the melted butter. Mix in well. Set aside to rest for approximately 35 minutes.

3 Peel and slice the carrots finely. Cut the slices into thin matchsticks.

4 Trim the ends of the courgettes. Cut into chunks, slices and then into matchsticks.

5 Shell the peas and the broad beans. Steam together for 10 minutes, beginning with the peas, and 3 minutes later adding the beans. After cooking, remove the skins of the broad beans.

6 Steam the carrots for 4 minutes and the courgettes for 3 minutes.

7 When the carrots and courgettes have cooked, steam the bean sprouts and the corn for 5 minutes. Remove and set aside.

8 Mix all the cooked vegetables together and season with salt and pepper. Add the remaining melted butter and mix in well so all the vegetables are coated. Set aside.

9 Fry the crepes lightly on each side in an oiled frying pan. Use kitchen paper to oil the pan lightly before pouring in the batter for each crepe.

10 Fill each crepe with some of the vegetable mixture. Fold up, and seal the folds with beaten egg.

11 In a saucepan reduce the white wine, shallots for 15 minutes. Whisk in the butter gradually. Add the chopped chives and a squeeze of lemon juice. Keep warm over hot water.

12 Reheat the crepes on a lightly buttered, non-stick baking tray in a warm oven for 10 minutes. Serve the filled crepes garnished with the chive-butter sauce. Garnish with chervil.

MIXED SEAFOOD FLAN

SERVES : 6

PREPARATION TIME : 45 Minutes
COOKING TIME : 35 Minutes

This is a seafood variation of the basic quiche. A pie shell is filled with a cheese custard and a mixture of mussels, shrimp and clams. Serve small slices as a first course or larger ones for a main dish, accompanied with a tossed green salad.

INGREDIENTS

- ☐ 250g/10oz flour
- ☐ 50ml/2 fl oz water
- ☐ 1 egg yolk
- ☐ 125g/5oz butter at room temperature
- ☐ 1 litre/2 pints mussels
- ☐ 500g/1lb cockles
- ☐ 200ml/8 fl oz white wine
- ☐ 200g/8oz medium cooked prawns
- ☐ 300g/12oz small scallops
- ☐ 200ml/8 fl oz milk
- ☐ 300ml/12 fl oz cream
- ☐ 4 eggs
- ☐ 100g/4oz grated Gruyère cheese
- ☐ Nutmeg
- ☐ Butter
- ☐ Fresh herbs (dill)
- ☐ Salt and pepper

1 Make the pastry by mixing together the flour, the water, salt and egg yolk

2 Add the softened butter, and mix into the dough completely.

3 Work the pastry dough into a ball, and allow to rest in the refrigerator for 30 minutes.

4 Rinse and rub clean the mussels and cockles. Use several changes of water to eliminate all the sand.

5 Place the mussels and cockles in separate saucepans, each containing half of the wine. Cover and cook until the shells open, approximately 5 minutes. Allow to cool.

6 Shell the prawns. Cut into small pieces. Wash the scallops, and discard the coral. Remove the mussels and cockles from their shells.

7 In a bowl, mix together the milk, cream, eggs, grated cheese, salt, pepper, and a few gratings of nutmeg. Set aside.

8 Roll out the pastry on a lightly floured surface using a floured rolling pin.

9 Use the pastry to line a greased flan dish. Trim off the excess pastry. Prick the base of the pastry with a fork.

10 Drain all excess liquid from the seafood. Arrange with the uncooked sea scallops in the bottom of the pastry case.

11 Pour over the custard mixture, and cook in a very hot oven (240°C/475°F/Gas Mark 9) for 25 minutes. Cover with a sheet of foil, if necessary.

12 Remove from the flan case, and serve warm, cut into wedges. Accompany with a tossed, mixed lettuce salad, if desired. Garnish with dill.

STUFFED EGGS À LA PROVENÇALE

SERVES : 6

PREPARATION TIME : 40 Minutes
COOKING TIME : 30 Minutes

Hard-boiled eggs are halved and filled with the yolks mixed with anchovies. Provençale ingredients traditionally include garlic and tomatoes. In this case it refers to the vegetable side dish of onion, peppers and tomatoes.

INGREDIENTS

- ☐ 9 eggs
- ☐ 6 anchovy fillets (in oil)
- ☐ 4 peppers (2 red, 2 green)
- ☐ 2 onions
- ☐ 2 cloves garlic (central shoot removed)
- ☐ 1 chilli pepper
- ☐ 1 egg yolk
- ☐ 1 tsp mustard
- ☐ ¼ litre/½ pint olive oil
- ☐ 8 green olives
- ☐ 1 tbsp wine vinegar
- ☐ Fresh herbs (chervil)
- ☐ Salt and pepper

1 Hard-boil the eggs for 10 minutes. Cool in cold water.

2 Shell the eggs, cut in half lengthwise and remove the yolks, with a stainless steel knife. Press the yolks through a fine sieve. Set aside the whites.

3 Bone the anchovy fillets if necessary and push them through a fine sieve. Set aside.

4 Cut, open the peppers, and remove all seeds and pith. Cut into even-sized slices.

5 Peel and chop the onions with the garlic. Slice open the chilli pepper and remove the seeds.

9 Stone the olives, and chop finely.

6 Fry the onion, half of the garlic, the chilli pepper and peppers in 50ml/2 fl oz olive oil for 15 minutes, stirring frequently. Season with salt and pepper, and set aside to cool.

10 Stir the cooked egg yolks, the anchovy paste, and the chopped olives into the mayonnaise. Beat in the vinegar.

7 Make the mayonnaise. Mix together one raw egg yolk, the mustard, salt and pepper. Whisk in the remaining oil gradually.

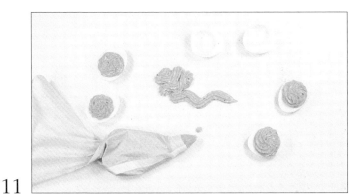

11 Place the mixture in a piping bag and fill the egg halves, decoratively.

8 Add the remaining chopped garlic to the mayonnaise. Mix in well and chill.

12 Serve the stuffed eggs atop the cooled pepper and onion mixture (remove the chilli pepper). Garnish with the chervil leaves.

LASAGNE

WITH

SEAFOOD

SERVES : 6

PREPARATION TIME : 1 Hour 30 Minutes
COOKING TIME : 1 Hour 15 Minutes

Home-made lasagne pasta is layered with mussels, cockles and prawns in an aromatic tomato sauce and topped with grated Swiss cheese. This dish can be prepared in advance and reheated. If time is short, use commercially prepared lasagne sheets.

INGREDIENTS

- ☐ 400g/1lb flour
- ☐ 4 eggs
- ☐ 4 tbsps olive oil
- ☐ 400g/1lb cockles
- ☐ 1 litre/2 pints mussels
- ☐ 300g/12oz prawns
- ☐ 200ml/8 fl oz white wine
- ☐ 2 shallots, chopped
- ☐ 1 onion, finely chopped
- ☐ 2 cloves garlic, chopped
- ☐ 6 tomatoes, skinned, seeded and crushed
- ☐ 2 tbsps chopped parsley
- ☐ 40g/1½oz butter, melted
- ☐ 100g/4oz gruyère, grated
- ☐ Fresh herbs (chervil)
- ☐ Salt and pepper

1 In a bowl, mix together the flour, 1 tsp salt and the eggs with your fingers to form into a dough. Shape into a ball.

2 Divide the dough into 4 and flatten each piece before passing it through the rollers of a pasta machine.

3 Continue rolling until long, thin strips of pasta are formed. Flour frequently during the process. Cut into small rectangles and leave to dry for 2 hours.

4 Cook the lasagne sheets a few at a time in boiling, salted water with 1 tbsp of oil, for 3 minutes each.

5 Remove and refresh under cold water, then lay on a damp tea towel until needed.

6 Wash and scrub the cockles and mussels. Change the water often as you wash. Peel the prawns and cut into pieces.

7 Pour the wine into a casserole, add the shallots, cockles, and cook, covered, on a high heat until they open. Remove. Cook the mussels in the same liquid until they open. Shell both.

8 Fry the onions and garlic in 3 tbsps olive oil in a frying pan. Add the tomato and 1 tbsp parsley. Strain the stock from the shellfish through a sieve lined with muslin.

9 Add the prawns, cockles and mussels, with their cooking liquid, to the pan. Cook over a moderate heat for 20 minutes.

10 Brush an ovenproof baking dish with some of the butter. Layer the sheets of lasagne with the seafood mixture. Brush the pasta with butter each time.

11 Finish with a layer of lasagne, brush with butter. Sprinkle over the cheese and remaining parsley. Cover with foil and bake in a hot oven (220°C/450°F/Gas Mark 6) for 25 minutes.

12 Remove the foil. Brown the top of the lasagna under a broiler for 5 minutes. Serve cut into portions, garnished with the chopped chervil.

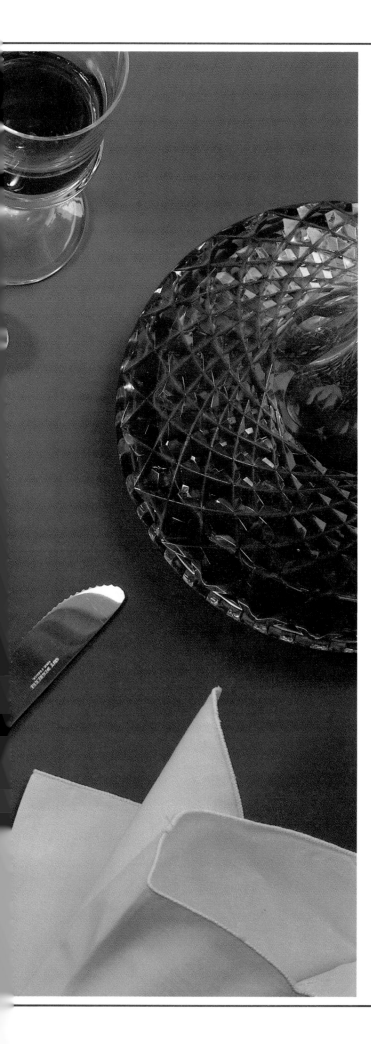

SPAGHETTI

WITH

CRAB AND BACON

SERVES : 6

PREPARATION TIME : 1 Hour
COOKING TIME : 20 Minutes

This recipe includes a wonderful preparation of home-made parsley pasta. It is tossed and served with a seafood sauce, fresh or imitation crab and bacon.

INGREDIENTS

☐ 1 bunch parsley (approximately 6 tbsps)
☐ 500g/1lb 2oz flour
☐ 4 eggs
☐ 200g/8oz bacon, in one piece
☐ 1 tbsp olive oil
☐ 10 (300g/12oz) crab sticks, fresh or imitation
☐ 300ml/12 fl oz double cream
☐ 40g/1½oz butter
☐ Fresh herbs (chervil)
☐ Salt and pepper

1 Trim the leaves off the parsley. Cook for 10 minutes in boiling water. Pass through a fine sieve and reserve the cooking liquid.

2 Purée the parsley with 3 tbsps of the cooking liquid in a blender.

3 In a bowl, mix together the flour, salt, eggs and 1½ tbsps parsley purée. Form into a ball.

4 Quarter the dough and form these pieces into balls. Press each ball flat and run it through a pasta machine.

5 Thin the dough progressively by passing it through the machine several times. Flour the dough frequently throughout the operation.

6 Run the flattened strips of dough through the spaghetti cutter.

7 Cut the rind off the bacon and cut the bacon into strips, then cut into small rectangles.

8 Add the olive oil to boiling, salted water and cook the spaghetti for 5 minutes. Strain and rinse.

9 Shred the crab sticks with your fingers.

10 Heat the cream gently with the crab and bacon pieces.

11 Meanwhile, heat the butter in a pan and when it bubbles, add the spaghetti (first reheated by plunging for 30 seconds in boiling water). Mix well and season with salt and pepper.

12 Place the buttered spaghetti around the edges of the dinner plates and arrange the crab/bacon mixture in the centre. Garnish with chopped fresh herbs.

CHINESE NOODLES

WITH

VEGETABLES

SERVES : 6

PREPARATION TIME : 50 Minutes
COOKING TIME : 20 Minutes

*This is an Oriental-inspired vegetarian
preparation of Chinese noodles. They are mixed
with bamboo shoots, black mushrooms and
cucumber and a light sauce consisting of a
reduction of the cooking juices.*

INGREDIENTS

- ☐ 10g dried black Chinese mushrooms
- ☐ 1-inch piece fresh ginger root
- ☐ 1 clove garlic (central shoot removed)
- ☐ 2 carrots
- ☐ ¼ cucumber
- ☐ 200g/8oz bamboo shoots
- ☐ 100g/4oz bean sprouts
- ☐ 400g/14oz Chinese noodles
- ☐ 3 tbsps olive oil
- ☐ 1 small chilli pepper
- ☐ 5 tbsps soy sauce
- ☐ 1 tbsp honey
- ☐ Fresh herbs (chives)
- ☐ Salt and pepper

1 Soak the mushrooms for 15 minutes to reconstitute them. Trim off the sandy stump, and boil the mushrooms for 5 minutes.

2 Peel the ginger root with a vegetable peeler, cut off 3 slices, and chop finely. Chop the garlic finely.

3 Peel the carrots and cut into matchsticks. Squeeze out the water from the mushrooms, and slice into matchsticks.

4 Cut the cucumber into chunks. Work around the outside with a knife to obtain thick slices of peel, then cut the slices into matchsticks.

5 Trim the bamboo shoots. Cut into slices then into matchsticks.

6 Rinse, then blanch the bamboo shoots for 2 minutes. Set aside to drain thoroughly.

7 Trim, and wash the bean sprouts. Blanch for 1 minute. Plunge into cold water, and set aside to drain thoroughly.

8 Cook the noodles in boiling salted water for a few minutes, depending on the thickness of the noodles. Drain, rinse, and set aside to drain thoroughly.

9 In a frying pan, heat the oil, and fry the ginger, garlic and chilli pepper for several seconds.

10 Add the bamboo shoots, mushrooms and carrots. Fry for 4 minutes, then add the bean sprouts. Cook for another 2 minutes.

11 Add the noodles, soy sauce and honey. Stir well, and heat through.

12 At the last moment, add the cucumber. Heat for 1 minute. Remove the chilli pepper, garnish with the herbs, and serve.

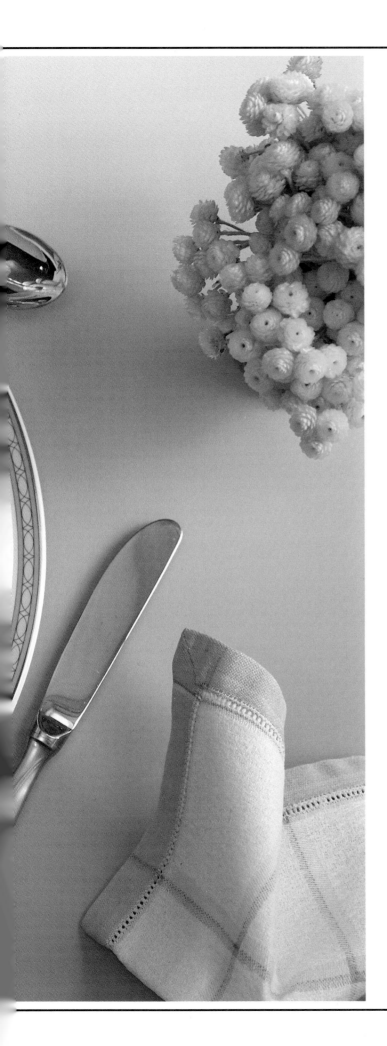

TAGLIATELLE

WITH

BLUE CHEESE

SERVES : 6

PREPARATION TIME : 1 Hour
COOKING TIME : 15 Minutes
DRYING : 2 Hours

Freshly made pasta noodles are tossed with a creamy sauce flavoured with blue cheese and diced dried apricots. The fruit and cheese mixture marries well to give a sweet and savoury dish. It is garnished with pine nuts to add texture and taste.

INGREDIENTS

- ☐ 500g/1lb 2oz flour
- ☐ 5 eggs
- ☐ 1 tbsp olive oil
- ☐ 100g/4oz blue cheese
  (Roquefort, Stilton)
- ☐ 100g/4oz dried apricots
  (or other dried fruit)
- ☐ 250ml/10 fl oz double cream
- ☐ 50ml/2 fl oz milk
- ☐ 2 egg yolks
- ☐ 50g/2oz pine nuts
- ☐ ½ bunch chives
- ☐ Salt and pepper

1 In a bowl, work together the flour, salt and eggs, to form a soft ball of dough.

2 Quarter and flatten each piece. Dredge each piece with plenty of flour. Flour the rollers of a pasta machine or a rolling pin, and either pass the dough through or roll it out.

3 Continue rolling the pasta until thin. Flour frequently during the process.

4 Thread the dough strips through the tagliatelle cutter, or cut into strips with a knife. Dredge the noodles with flour and allow to dry for 2 hours.

5 Bring to a boil a saucepan of salted water with 1 tbsp oil. Cook the pasta for 2 to 4 minutes, stirring with a fork.

6 Drain the tagliatelle and rinse in plenty of cold water to prevent sticking. Set aside.

7 Break up the cheese and force through a sieve with the back of a spoon.

8 Cut the apricots into strips then dice.

9 Slowly heat the cream in a saucepan. Stir in the cheese and milk. Blend until smooth with a hand held electric mixer.

10 Whilst the sauce is hot, stir in the tagliatelle, apricots, and season again, as necessary. Heat through quickly, so the cream does not curdle not the noodles overcook.

11 Mix the pasta with two forks. Remove from the heat, and mix in the egg yolks and the pine nuts.

12 Chop the chives finely and sprinkle over the tagliatelle; serve immediately.

RABBIT RAVIOLI

WITH

TARRAGON

SERVES : 6

PREPARATION TIME : 1 Hour 30 Minutes
COOKING TIME : 1 Hour 50 Minutes

*A time-consuming pasta dish well worth the
effort. Home-made ravioli are filled with a
mixture of minced rabbit meat and fresh
tarragon. The light sauce is a reduction of the
cooking liquid enhanced with cream and
tarragon.*

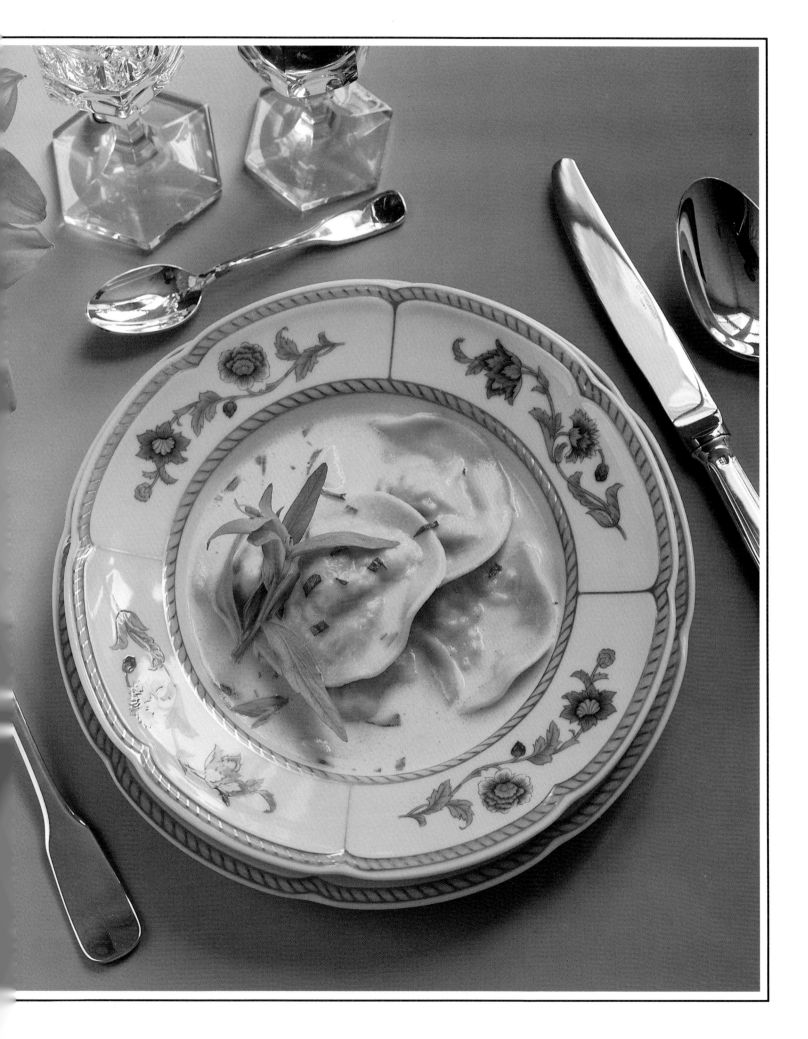

INGREDIENTS

- ☐ 300g/12oz flour
- ☐ 3 eggs
- ☐ ½ leek
- ☐ 1 onion, finely chopped
- ☐ 1 carrot
- ☐ 2 tbsps olive oil
- ☐ 3 rabbit thighs
- ☐ 5 sprigs tarragon
- ☐ 1 bouquet garni (parsley, thyme, bay leaf)
- ☐ 1 egg, beaten
- ☐ 50ml/2 fl oz double cream
- ☐ Salt and pepper

1 Place the flour in a bowl with 1 tsp salt. Add the eggs. Mix with your fingers to make a dough and form into a ball. Set aside to rest.

2 Wash and dice the leek, onion and carrot. Set aside.

3 Fry the rabbit in the oil until lightly coloured.

4 Remove the tarragon leaves from three sprigs, reserve the stalks for the stock, and chop the leaves.

5 Add the onion, carrot, leek, tarragon stalks and bouquet garni to the rabbit. Cook for 2 minutes. Add ³/₄ litre/1¹/₂ pints water. Cook covered on a low heat for 1 hour 30 minutes.

6 When cooked, remove the rabbit thighs, bone, and mince the meat. Mix with ³/₄ of the tarragon leaves. Season with salt and pepper. Strain the stock through a fine sieve and set it aside.

7 Divide the dough into smaller, flat rounds, and thread these through a pasta machine to form thin pasta strips.

8 Cut the pasta into rectangles. Mix 2 tbsps stock into the meat and tarragon, and place about a teaspoon of the mixture in the centre of each rectangle.

9 Brush the edges of the rectangles with beaten egg and fold over one side. Pinch the edges together with your fingers, then, using a pastry cutter, shape into rounds. Set aside.

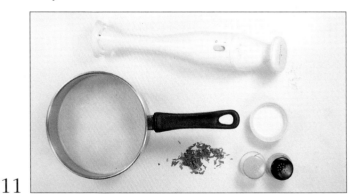

10 Cook the ravioli for 5 minutes in salted, boiling water with 1 sprig tarragon. Drain with a slotted spoon, then place on a damp tea towel.

11 Reduce 300ml/12 fl oz rabbit stock by half, add the cream and remaining tarragon. Blend smooth, heat through and season.

12 Serve the ravioli and cream sauce in soup plates. Garnish with the chopped tarragon.

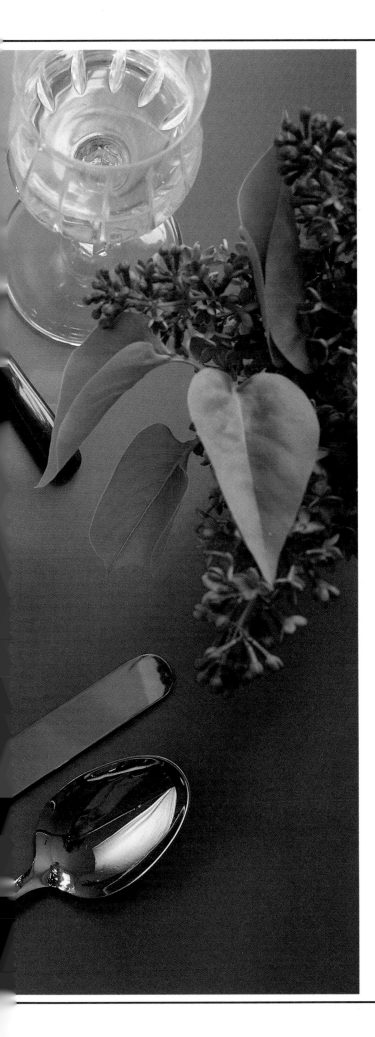

PASTA

WITH

LEEKS

AND MUSSELS

SERVES : 6

PREPARATION TIME : 30 Minutes
COOKING TIME : 25 Minutes

This pasta dish is relatively quick and easy to prepare. Spiral-shaped pasta is tossed with cooked mussels and sautéed leeks and a sauce of the reduced cooking juices. The thinly sliced ham adds flavour and makes an attractive garnish.

INGREDIENTS

- ☐ 1¹/₂ litre/3 pints mussels
- ☐ 100ml/4 fl oz white wine
- ☐ 1 shallot, chopped
- ☐ 2 medium-sized leeks
- ☐ 150ml/6 fl oz double cream
- ☐ 500g/1lb spiral-shaped pasta
- ☐ 1 tbsp oil
- ☐ 2 slices ham
- ☐ 15g/¹/₂ oz butter
- ☐ Fresh herbs (chives)
- ☐ Salt and pepper

1 Scrub the mussels; remove the "beard" and wash in several changes of water to eliminate the sand.

2 In a large, covered saucepan, cook the mussels in the white wine with the chopped shallot for approximately 5 minutes, over a high heat.

3 Cool, and remove the opened mussels from their shells. Reserve the cooking liquid.

4 Quarter each leek lengthwise, wash thoroughly, and slice finely.

5

In a covered saucepan, cook the leeks in the cream with salt and pepper to taste for 10 minutes over a low heat.

6

In a large casserole of water, boil the pasta with 1 tbsp oil. Stir the pasta as it cooks, to prevent sticking.

7

Drain after 5 or 6 minutes. Rinse in cold water to prevent sticking.

8

Remove any fat or rind from the ham, and slice into small pieces.

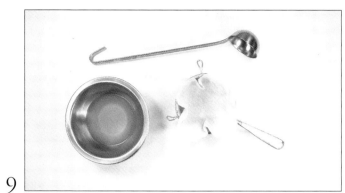

9

Strain the mussel cooking liquid through a sieve lined with muslin. Measure out approximately 100ml/4 fl oz.

10

Add the shelled mussels and the mussel liquid to the cream mixture, and cook for 4 minutes, stirring constantly.

11

Melt the butter in a deep frying pan, and reheat the pasta gently with the ham. Season to taste.

12

When the pasta is heated through, add the cream and leek sauce, and serve garnished with the chopped chives.

POTATO

AND

LAMB CASSEROLE AU GRATIN

SERVES : 6

PREPARATION TIME : 45 Minutes
COOKING TIME : 1 Hour 30 Minutes

*A wonderful lunch or supper dish which can be
prepared ahead and reheated. Sliced potatoes
are layered with a filling of ground lamb and
onion, topped with grated Swiss cheese and
browned in the oven. Serve hot or at room
temperature with a green salad.*

INGREDIENTS

- [ ] 1kg/2½lbs potatoes
- [ ] 500g/1¼lbs lamb shoulder, boned
- [ ] 1 egg
- [ ] 1 clove garlic (central shoot removed)
- [ ] 4 sprigs parsley
- [ ] 50ml/2 fl oz milk
- [ ] 2 tomatoes
- [ ] 2 onions
- [ ] 4 slices white bread
- [ ] 2 tbsps olive oil
- [ ] 50ml/2 fl oz/chicken or vegetable stock
- [ ] 100g/4oz Gruyère cheese, grated
- [ ] 4 servings mixed lettuce, washed and trimmed
- [ ] 4 tbsps vinaigrette sauce
- [ ] Fresh basil (optional)
- [ ] Salt and pepper

1 Peel the potatoes and slice them very thinly. Use a grater if available.

2 Cut the lamb in pieces. Place the meat in a food processor with the egg, and season with salt and pepper. Process finely.

3 Chop the garlic finely. Wash, trim and finely chop the parsley.

4 Add the garlic and parsley to the meat. Add the milk and mix well.

5 Cut the core out of the tomatoes and slice thinly with a serrated knife.

9 Add a layer of the tomato mixture with half of the onion.

6 Peel and cut the onions in half. Slice very thinly. Set aside.

10 Add the meat mixture, then the remaining onion. Pour in the stock.

7 Place the bread in a food processor, and process to obtain fine breadcrumbs.

11 Layer the remaining potato over the meat and onion. Top with the breadcrumbs and cheese. Cover with foil, cook in a hot oven (220°C/425°F/Gas Mark 7) for 1 hour 30 minutes.

8 Oil the base of a gratin dish (or ovenproof baking dish), and distribute half of the potato. Season well.

12 Halfway through the baking period, remove the foil. Serve with a tossed, mixed green salad dressed with a classic vinaigrette. Decorate with the fresh basil, if desired.

BAKED POTATO PANCAKE

WITH

RATATOUILLE

SERVES : 6

PREPARATION TIME : 50 Minutes
COOKING TIME : 25 Minutes

This dish is rather elaborate to prepare, but makes an original and delicious vegetarian starter or luncheon dish. Thinly sliced potatoes are filled with a flavourful vegetable preparation of onion, aubergine and tomato, and baked in the oven.

INGREDIENTS

- ☐ 1 onion
- ☐ 1 clove garlic (central shoot removed)
- ☐ 1 aubergine
- ☐ 2 courgettes
- ☐ 2 peppers (1 red and 1 green)
- ☐ 2 tomatoes
- ☐ 4 tbsps olive oil
- ☐ Bouquet garni (parsley, thyme, bay leaf)
- ☐ 1 egg
- ☐ 1kg/2¼lbs medium potatoes
- ☐ Salt and pepper

1 Peel and slice the onion finely. Halve the garlic, remove the central shoot and chop finely.

2 Trim the courgettes and aubergine. Cut into slices, sticks then cubes.

3 Cut open the peppers, remove all white pith and seeds, and dice.

4 Remove the stalks of the tomatoes. Plunge for 10 seconds in boiling water. Refresh immediately in cold water.

5 Peel off the skins, halve, seed and roughly chop.

9 Oil a frying pan, and arrange half of the potatoes in a neat rose shape. Season with salt and pepper.

6 In a frying pan, heat 2 tbsps of oil and fry the garlic; add the diced vegetables (except the tomatoes) and cook for 5 minutes, stirring. Add the tomato and bouquet garni.

10 Spread the ratatouille over the potatoes, covering well.

7 Season the ratatouille with salt and pepper. After 10 minutes, the liquid should have evaporated. Cool, then stir in the egg. Set aside.

11 Cover the ratatouille with another layer of potatoes. Bake, uncovered, in a hot oven (200°C/400°F/Gas Mark 6) for 20 minutes.

8 Peel and rinse the potatoes. Trim into smooth cylinder shapes. Slice thinly with a knife or a grater.

12 Remove from the oven and turn out onto a serving plate. Serve as a first course with a tossed salad, or as a side dish with meat.

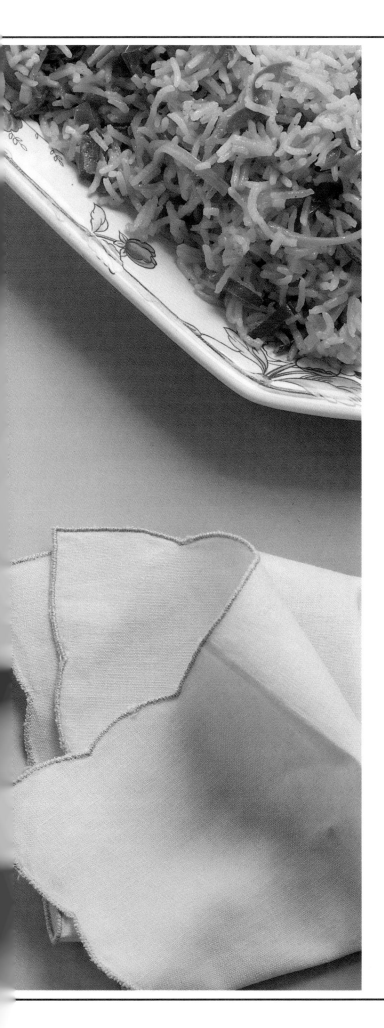

BASMATI RICE

WITH

VEGETABLES

SERVES : 6

PREPARATION TIME : 45 Minutes
COOKING TIME : 30 Minutes

*A vegetarian rice dish which can be served by
itself or as an accompaniment to meat and fish.
The rice is mixed with diced carrots, courgette
and peppers, and is flavoured with exotic
Indian spices. (The basmati rice can be replaced
with ordinary rice, but the taste is not as good.)*

INGREDIENTS

- [ ] 2 peppers (1 green, 1 red)
- [ ] 1 courgette
- [ ] 1 carrot
- [ ] 2 shallots
- [ ] ½ vanilla pod
- [ ] 2 pinches cinnamon
- [ ] 1 pinch saffron
- [ ] ½ tsp turmeric
- [ ] ½ tsp curry powder
- [ ] 3 cardamom seeds
- [ ] 3 tbsps olive oil
- [ ] 300g/12oz basmati rice
- [ ] 1 bouquet garni (parsley, thyme, bay leaf)
- [ ] Fresh chervil
- [ ] Salt and pepper

1 Trim the stem from the peppers, remove all white pith and seeds.

2 Cut peppers into even-sized strips.

3 Cut the courgette into chunks, then slices, and finally matchsticks.

4 Cut the carrot into slightly smaller matchsticks.

5 Peel the shallots, halve lengthwise, and chop finely.

6 Slit open the vanilla pod, run the back of the knife down the inside to extract the seeds. Tie the parsley, thyme and bay leaf into a bouquet garni.

7 Mix together the spices, cinnamon, saffron, turmeric, curry powder, cardamom, and vanilla pod.

8 In an ovenproof frying pan, heat the oil and sauté the vegetables for 5 minutes, stirring frequently, with a spatula.

9 When cooked through, add the rice and bouquet garni.

10 Fry the rice until transparent. Measure water 1½ times the volume of the rice and stir the spices into the water.

11 Add the water and spices to the rice (do not stir again). Cover and cook in a hot oven (220°C/425°F/Gas Mark 7) for 25 minutes.

12 Fluff the rice with a fork and serve garnished with the chervil.

RICE PILAF

WITH

MIXED SEAFOOD

SERVES : 6

PREPARATION TIME : 45 Minutes
COOKING TIME : 40 Minutes

Rice is cooked pilaf style in a seafood stock. It is mixed with a variety of seafood and a creamy herb sauce. The different seafoods can be varied according to your taste and the availability of fresh ingredients.

INGREDIENTS

☐ 2 shallots
☐ 150g/6oz mushrooms
☐ 250ml/10 fl oz white wine
☐ 6 large clams, well washed
☐ 1 litre/2 pints mussels, well washed
☐ 5 sprigs of parsley
☐ 500g/1¼lbs cockles, well washed
☐ 12 small clams, well washed
☐ 40g/1½oz butter
☐ 600g/1lb 6oz long grain rice
☐ 250ml/10 fl oz double cream
☐ Fresh herbs (chervil)
☐ Salt and pepper

1 Peel and slice the shallots crosswise. Trim, wash and slice the mushrooms finely.

2 In a frying pan, cook the shallots with the clams and the white wine, covered, until the clams open.

3 Remove the clams. Leave the liquid in the pan. Add the mussels and cook, covered, until the shells open.

4 Meanwhile, trim, wash, dry and finely chop the leaves of the parsley. Set aside.

5 Remove the mussels from the frying pan when opened, and cook the cockles in the same liquid, covered, until they open.

9 In a frying pan, heat the butter and fry together the shellfish, mushrooms and the rice, shaking the pan continuously. Cook for 2 minutes over a high heat.

6 Remove the opened cockles and cook the small clams, covered, in the same liquid until open.

10 Pour into the frying pan water or fish stock equal to 1¹/₂ times the volume of the rice. Season, cover and cook in hot oven (220⁰C/425⁰F/Gas Mark 7) for 25 minutes.

7 Remove the shellfish from the shells. Cut out the intestinal bags from the larger fish, if necessary. Rinse well to eliminate sand.

11 Reduce the cooking liquid from the shellfish for 1 minute over a medium heat. Add the cream and reduce for 2 minutes more. Blend the mixture smooth and add the parsley.

8 Strain the cooking liquid through a muslin-lined sieve, discard the impurities and set aside the stock.

12 Serve the rice and the shellfish in a mound with the sauce poured around the edge. Decorate with the chervil.

SALT COD

WITH

PEPPERS

SERVES : 6

PREPARATION TIME : 50 Minutes
COOKING TIME : 1 Hour 20 Minutes
SOAKING TIME : 24 Hours

This dish is based on a traditional Portuguese country recipe using potato, cod and tomato. It has been modernized and refined in an elegant preparation of layered puréed potato, cod and ratatouille.

INGREDIENTS

☐ 1kg/2lbs salt cod
☐ 4 peppers (2 red, 2 green)
☐ 3 large onions
☐ 6 cloves garlic
☐ 1 small red chilli pepper
☐ 5 large potatoes
☐ 3 tbsps olive oil
☐ 4 tbsps double cream
☐ 2 tbsps chopped parsley
☐ 2 tomatoes, peeled, seeded and chopped
☐ Fresh herbs (chervil)
☐ Salt and pepper

1 Cut the salt cod into pieces. Soak in water for 24 hours, changing the water several times.

2 Cut open the peppers, remove the seeds and white pith. Slice.

3 Peel and chop the onions finely. Cut the garlic cloves in half and remove the central shoot. Chop the garlic. Seed and chop the chilli pepper.

4 Peel the potatoes. Quarter them and cook in boiling salted water with 1 chopped onion and 1 tbsp of olive oil for 30 minutes.

5 Drain the potatoes and onions when cooled. Blend smooth or press through a sieve. Add the cream, and parsley and season to taste.

9 Add the peppers and the two remaining onions. Cook for 10 minutes over a moderate heat, stirring well.

6 Bring to a boil the soaked and drained cod in a large quantity of water and cook for 5 minutes.

10 Add the tomato to the peppers and onions, and cook for another 15 minutes, stirring frequently. Season to taste.

7 Set aside to drain and cool. Flake with your fingers, discarding the skin and bones.

11 Oil the bottom of an ovenproof dish. Arrange a layer of the potato purée over the bottom. Spread over the cod.

8 Fry the chopped garlic and chilli pepper in the remaining oil until soft and lightly coloured.

12 Top with a layer of the pepper, onion and tomato mixture. Bake in a hot oven (200°C/400°F/Mark 6) for 30 minutes. Serve hot, garnished with the chopped chervil.

MINUTE SALMON

WITH

VANILLA

VINAIGRETTE

SERVES : 6

PREPARATION TIME : 30 Minutes
COOKING TIME : 15 Minutes

An unusual and surprisingly tasty flavour combination; quickly sautéed, thinly sliced salmon and cooked French beans are served with a vanilla vinaigrette. This dish can be served as a starter or as a cold main course.

INGREDIENTS

- ☐ 1 salmon (2½ lbs approximately)
- ☐ 300g/12oz French beans
- ☐ 2 shallots
- ☐ ½ vanilla pod
- ☐ 1 tbsp wine vinegar
- ☐ 4 tbsps oil
- ☐ 1 bunch chives
- ☐ Fresh dill
- ☐ 1 egg
- ☐ 2 tbsps olive oil
- ☐ 15g/½oz butter
- ☐ Salt and pepper

1 Fillet the salmon using a sharp knife. Remove any bones with a vegetable peeler.

2 Cut each strip of salmon into 3 pieces, slicing at an angle.

3 Wash and trim the French beans. Cook in salted, boiling water for 8 to 10 minutes.

4 Drain, then rinse the beans. Slice them into very thin strips.

5 Peel the shallots, cut them in two, lengthwise, then chop finely. Cut open the vanilla pod and remove the seeds by scraping with the back of a knife.

6 To make the sauce, mix together the salt, pepper, vinegar. Allow to dissolve then add the vanilla seeds and shallots. Whisk in the oil.

7 Chop the chives finely. Trim and chop the dill leaves. Set aside.

8 Beat the egg in a ramekin and brush the salmon pieces on both sides. Season.

9 Sprinkle the salmon with the chopped chives (reserving some for the presentation), and season again.

10 Heat the olive oil in a frying pan and add the butter. When the butter is bubbling, sear the fish for 40 seconds on each side.

11 Mix the French beans in a bowl with the vinaigrette dressing.

12 Drain the lightly cooked salmon on kitchen paper. Serve immediately with the French beans and vinaigrette. Garnish with the chopped herbs (dill and chives).

SCALLOPS
À LA NAGE
WITH LEEKS
AND TRUFFLES

SERVES : 6

PREPARATION TIME : 35 Minutes
COOKING TIME : 20 Minutes

*A rich and expensive dish which deserves
special occasions. Fresh scallops swim in a thin
cream sauce with sautéed leeks and sliced black
truffles. The costly truffles, found in speciality
food shops, can be reduced in quantity or
eliminated, since there is no substitute.*

INGREDIENTS

- [ ] 18 scallops in their shells
- [ ] 3 medium leeks
- [ ] 25g/1oz butter
- [ ] 250ml/10 fl oz fish stock
- [ ] 2 truffles, brushed clean
- [ ] 200ml/8 fl oz double cream
- [ ] Fresh herbs (chervil, chives)
- [ ] Salt and pepper

1 Open the scallops. With the tip of a sharp knife, prising off the top shell.

2 When open, slip the knife in under the scallop and cut it out from the shell.

3 Remove the fleshy, "bearded" parts from around the scallop. Discard. Save the coral for another dish.

4 Rinse the scallops, removing all sand. Dry on a tea towel.

5 Cut the roots off the leeks. Cut them in 4 lengthwise. Wash carefully and shred finely.

6 Melt the butter in a deep saucepan and add the leek. Cook, stirring, for 1 minute.

7 Pour over the stock, season with salt and pepper and cook on a simmer for 15 minutes.

8 Slice the scallops crosswise in 2 or 3 pieces and add them to the saucepan. Cook 1 minute.

9 Cut the truffles into even-sized rounds and then into very thin matchstick slices.

10 Add the cream, truffles and truffle juice to the leeks and scallops. Cook for 5 minutes.

11 Meanwhile, wash and dry the chives and the chervil leaves. Chop finely.

12 Serve the scallops and sauce hot, garnished with the chopped herbs.

INGREDIENTS

- ☐ 1 carrot
- ☐ ½ leek
- ☐ 2 shallots
- ☐ 1 onion
- ☐ 2 tbsps olive oil
- ☐ 1kg/2lbs fish bones and trimmings
- ☐ 4 fennel bulbs
- ☐ Juice of 1 lemon
- ☐ 300ml/12 fl oz double cream
- ☐ 1kg/2lbs salmon fillets
- ☐ ½ bunch chives
- ☐ Salt and pepper

1 Peel, wash and chop the carrot, leek, shallots and onion.

2 In a casserole, heat the oil and cook the chopped vegetables. Add the fish bones and trimmings, and sauté for 5 minutes.

3 Add water to cover, with 1 tsp salt and boil for 20 minutes. Skim the top of the water from time to time.

4 Trim the fennel and chop two of the bulbs very finely. Use a food processor, if available.

5 Cook the fennel for 3 minutes in salted, boiling water with the lemon juice. Drain and refresh in cold water.

9 Place the two remaining fennel bulbs in a juice extractor, or blend in a food processor and strain the juice. Reserve the juice.

6 Place the fennel in a saucepan with half the cream, season, cover and cook gently for 10 minutes.

10 Strain the fish stock through a fine sieve lined with muslin. Measure off ¼ litre/½ pint. Cook the salmon millefeuilles in a hot oven (200⁰C/400⁰F/Gas Mark 6) for 10 minutes.

7 Cut the salmon into thin slices with a serrated knife. Season.

11 Reduce the stock by half, add the remaining cream, boil for 2 minutes. Add the fennel juice at the last moment. Blend smooth with a hand-held electric mixer. Season.

8 In 6 metal rings (on greaseproof paper) or greased ramekins alternate the salmon with the fennel mixture.

12 Run a knife around the sides of the salmon millefeuilles, turn out and serve with the sauce. Sprinkle with the chopped chives.

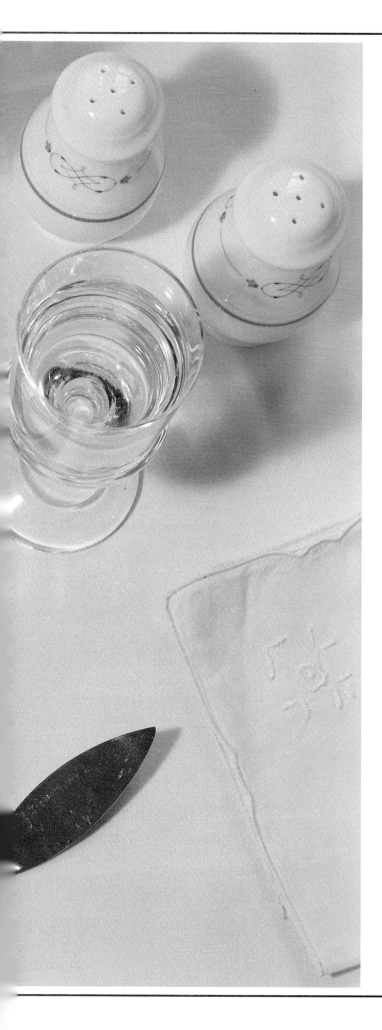

OCEAN PERCH

AND

KING PRAWN DUET

SERVES : 6

PREPARATION TIME : 30 Minutes
COOKING TIME : 35 Minutes

Ratatouille vegetables of onion, aubergine, courgette and tomato are slowly cooked, then puréed, and topped with steamed fish and large king prawns sautéed in olive oil. This tasty fish dish is elegant, yet low in calories.

INGREDIENTS

- [ ] 18 raw king prawns
- [ ] 800g/2lbs ocean perch fillets
- [ ] 1 pepper ($\frac{1}{2}$ red and $\frac{1}{2}$ green)
- [ ] 1 onion
- [ ] 1 tomato, peeled and seeded
- [ ] 1 courgette
- [ ] 5 tbsps olive oil
- [ ] 1 clove garlic
- [ ] 1 bouquet garni (parsley, thyme, bay leaf)
- [ ] 250ml/10 fl oz fish stock
- [ ] Fresh herbs (chervil)
- [ ] Salt and pepper

1 Peel the prawns and remove their heads and tails.

2 Cut down the back of the prawns, devein them and cut them in two, lengthwise.

3 Cut the perch fillets into even, bite-sized pieces.

4 Remove the pith and seeds from the peppers and slice them thinly. Peel and chop the onion finely.

5 Chop the tomato to obtain a pulp. Cut the garlic in half, and remove the central shoot.

6 Trim the ends of the courgette, wash and cut into thin rounds.

7 In 3 tbsps of olive oil, fry the onion and the peppers for 3 minutes. Add the garlic, courgette and the tomato pulp. Mix well.

8 After frying for 5 minutes, add the bouquet garni, salt, pepper and the fish stock. Cover and cook over a moderate heat for 20 minutes, stirring frequently.

9 Heat 2 tbsps of olive oil and sear the prawns evenly all over for 3 minutes. Season with salt and pepper. Drain on kitchen paper and keep warm in the oven.

10 Place the fish fillets in a steamer. Season with salt and pepper, and cook, covered, for 5 minutes.

11 Remove the bouquet garni from the vegetable mixture and blend to a smooth purée with a hand-held electric mixer.

12 Serve the fish fillets and prawns with the vegetable purée sauce, garnished with the fresh herbs (chervil).

RED MULLET

WITH

NUTMEG

SERVES : 6

PREPARATION TIME : 1 Hour
COOKING TIME : 50 Minutes

*For this original fish dish, courgette "galettes"
are prepared much like potato pancakes, then
decoratively topped with sautéed fish fillets and
served in a nutmeg-flavoured cream sauce.*

INGREDIENTS

- ☐ 2 red mullet (1kg/2½lbs each)
- ☐ 8 courgettes
- ☐ 1 egg
- ☐ 1 tbsp crème fraîche or double cream
- ☐ 5 tbsps olive oil
- ☐ 100ml/4 fl oz rich fish stock
- ☐ 300ml/12 fl oz double cream
- ☐ 1 nutmeg
- ☐ ½ lemon
- ☐ 2 tbsps butter
- ☐ ½ bunch chives, chopped
- ☐ Salt and pepper

1 Cut the fins off the red mullet with a pair of scissors.

2 Scrape off the scales with a fish scaler or the blade of a sharp knife. Gut and rinse well.

3 With a sharp knife, cut off the fillets, running the knife carefully down the backbone.

4 Using a vegetable grater, slice the courgettes into thin julienne. Discard the soft seed centre.

5 In a bowl, beat the eggs with the crème fraîche, salt, pepper and then add the courgettes. Mix thoroughly with a fork.

6 In a small ovenproof frying pan, heat 1 tbsp of oil and fry ⅓ of the courgette mixture, flattening it into a pancake shape.

7 After about 3 minutes turn over the courgette/galette and finish cooking it in a hot oven (200°C/400°F/Gas Mark 6). Repeat the process three times.

8 Reduce the stock by half, then stir in the double cream, 6 or 7 scrapings of nutmeg, salt and pepper. Boil for 1 minute.

9 Remove from the heat, blend smooth with a hand held electric mixer, add a few drops of lemon juice and keep warm in a bowl of hot water.

10 Season the red mullet fillets with salt and pepper and a few scrapings of nutmeg.

11 In 2 tbsps of oil melt the butter and fry the red mullet fillets on both sides until lightly coloured. Finish cooking in a hot oven (200ºC/400ºF/Gas Mark 6) for 8 minutes.

12 Cut the galettes into 8 pieces, spread the pieces out on a plate, lay the fillets over and pour over the sauce. Sprinkle on the chopped chives.

GRILLED SEA BASS

WITH

FENNEL

AND ANISEED

SERVES : 6

PREPARATION TIME : 40 Minutes
COOKING TIME : 30 Minutes
MARINADE : 1 Hour

*Fennel, an aniseed-flavoured plant of Italian
origin, is sautéed in butter and served with
grilled fish fillets. It is topped with a puréed and
lightly creamed tomato and shallot sauce and
garnished with fresh dill.*

INGREDIENTS

- [ ] 6 small sea bass
- [ ] Juice of ½ lemon
- [ ] 1 tbsp aniseed
- [ ] 3 tbsps olive oil
- [ ] 3 fennel bulbs
- [ ] ½ litre/1 pint milk
- [ ] 2 shallots
- [ ] 2 tomatoes
- [ ] 300ml/12 fl oz rich fish stock
- [ ] 200ml/8 fl oz double cream
- [ ] 2 tbsps butter
- [ ] Fresh herbs (dill)
- [ ] Salt and pepper

1 Scale and gut the sea bass. Remove the fillets by cutting down the backbone.

2 Cut each of the fillets in two, to obtain 4 small fillets per person. Season with salt and pepper.

3 Mix together the lemon juice, aniseed and 2 tbsps olive oil. Add the fish fillets, and marinate for 1 hour, turning from time to time.

4 Wash, trim and slice the fennel. Discard the hard centre core.

5 Bring the milk to a boil. Add salt and the fennel slices and cook for 5 minutes. Drain, then spread to dry on a tea towel.

6 Peel and finely chop the shallot. Cut the tomatoes in half, squeeze to extract the pips. Chop roughly.

7 Drain the marinade into a frying pan Add the shallots and tomato. Heat for 3 minutes, then add the fish stock. Reduce on a high heat for 5 minutes.

8 When reduced, add the cream and bring to a boil. Remove from the heat and blend smooth with a hand held electric mixer. Check seasoning.

9 Strain this sauce through a fine sieve, pushing through with a spoon to obtain a smooth sauce. Keep warm over boiling water Preheat a cast-iron griddle and grease it with a little oil.

10 Sear the fish fillets on each side, beginning skin side down. Place in an ovenproof dish and finish cooking in a hot oven (200°C/400°F/Gas Mark6) for 10 minutes.

11 Sauté the fennel in the remaining butter until lightly coloured. Season with salt and pepper.

12 Remove the fish from the oven. To serve, Top the fennel with the fish and the sauce. Garnish with fresh dill.

ROLLED FILLET
OF SOLE
WITH
CHICORY

SERVES : 6

PREPARATION TIME : 1 Hour
COOKING TIME : 20 Minutes

*A wonderful taste combination, flattened sole
fillets are filled with sliced bacon, rolled, then
steamed. They are served with sautéed chicory
and a lightly flavoured cream sauce.*

INGREDIENTS

- ☐ 3 sole
- ☐ 12 thin slices bacon
- ☐ 6 heads of chicory
- ☐ 300ml/12 fl oz double cream
- ☐ 40g/1½oz butter
- ☐ Fresh herbs (dill)
- ☐ Salt and pepper

1 Pull off the skins (white and black) off the sole. Use a cloth to help you hold the fish firmly.

2 Using a flexible knife, cut along the backbone and remove the fillets.

3 When you have removed the fillets, wrap them in cling film and press flat with the blade of a large chopping knife.

4 Cut the bacon slices to fit the fillets exactly. Save the trimmings. Season with pepper. Roll up neatly and tightly.

5 Place each roll on a piece of cling film. Fold it up and over the rolled fillets, twisting the two ends to close.

9 Heat the butter in a pan. When foaming, sauté the chicory over a high heat. It may be necessary to cook it in two batches.

6 Separate all the chicory leaves, wash, dry and cut in fine julienne, with a stainless-steel knife.

10 Season the chicory with salt and pepper. When cooked (approximately 3 minutes), set aside.

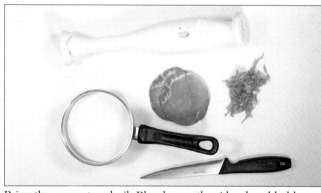

7 Bring the cream to a boil. Blend smooth with a hand held electric mixer, then add the bacon trimmings sliced finely. Keep warm over hot water.

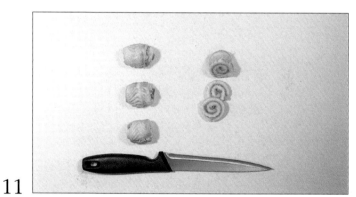

11 When the rolled fillets are cooked, remove the cling film and slice into round slices.

8 Cook the rolled fillets in a steamer for 10 minutes.

12 Place the slices on a bed of chicory with the reheated sauce. Sprinkle with chopped herbs (dill) and serve.

MARINATED RAW FISH

SERVES : 6

PREPARATION TIME : 40 Minutes
MARINADE : 10 Minutes

*This makes a lovely light entrée to any meal.
Thinly sliced salmon and whitefish fillets are
"cooked" in a lemon juice and olive oil
marinade flavoured with shallot and pepper
and served with sliced vegetables. It is essential
to this recipe that the fish, of whatever variety,
be exceptionally fresh.*

INGREDIENTS

- ☐ ½ small salmon (approximately 700g/1lb 8oz), halved lengthwise
- ☐ 1 fillet ocean perch or whitefish (approximately 300g/12oz)
- ☐ 1 carrot
- ☐ ½ cucumber
- ☐ 1 stick celery
- ☐ 2 shallots
- ☐ 2 sprigs dill
- ☐ 1 curly endive
- ☐ 2 lemons
- ☐ Mixed peppercorns in a pepper mill
- ☐ 4 tbsps olive oil
- ☐ 1 small jar lumpfish roe
- ☐ Salt and pepper

1 Slice the salmon very thinly with a sharp, serrated knife.

2 Arrange the slices around the rim of a serving platter, overlapping them.

3 Cut smaller slices of the ocean perch, proceeding as in step 1.

4 Interlace the perch slices with the salmon, working towards the centre of the platter.

5 Peel and cut the carrot into thin slices. Cut the slices into very thin julienne strips.

6 Cut the cucumber into chunks. Peel thickly, using a sharp knife. Discard the core. Cut the peel into julienne.

7 Peel the celery. Cut thin, even slices with a vegetable peeler. Cut into julienne.

8 Peel the shallots and halve them lengthwise. Finely and evenly chop the halves.

9 Wash and trim the curly endive and the dill. Discard the stalks of the dill and finely chop the leaves.

10 Squeeze the two lemons and mix the juice with the shallots and dill leaves.

11 Season the lemon juice and dill mixture with salt and a few turns of the pepper mill. Whisk in the olive oil.

12 Brush the sauce over all the fish. Marinate for 10 minutes and serve with the salad and julienned vegetables tossed in the remaining sauce. Garnish with the lumpfish roe.

RED MULLET

WITH

CELERY AND

CELERIAC

SERVES : 6

PREPARATION TIME : 40 Minutes
COOKING TIME : 20 Minutes

*Use a whole fish to carry out this recipe
correctly, since the liver is used to flavour the
sauce. The fillets are sautéed in butter with
parsley, and served with celery and celeriac
If using bought fillets, simply eliminate the liver
flavouring for the celery sauce.*

INGREDIENTS

- [ ] 12 small red mullet
- [ ] ½ large head celeriac
- [ ] 3 sticks celery
- [ ] 3 tbsps parsley
- [ ] ½ egg, beaten
- [ ] 150ml/6 fl oz rich fish stock
- [ ] 150ml/6 fl oz double cream
- [ ] 25g/1oz butter
- [ ] 2 tbsps olive oil
- [ ] Fresh herbs (chervil)
- [ ] Salt and pepper

1 Scale, gut and rinse the mullet. Remove the fillets, running the knife down the backbone.

2 Remove the livers from the mullet heads. Discard the bones and trimmings.

3 Peel the celeriac and cut into thin slices. Cut the slices into thin strips. Cut the celery sticks into slices.

4 Wash and dry the parsley, chop it very finely.

5 Season each fillet with salt and pepper, and brush the flesh side with beaten egg.

9 Strain the sauce through a muslin-lined sieve into a saucepan, pushing the mixture through. Add the cream and cook gently for 5 minutes. Set aside.

6 Dredge the side of fish covered with egg in the chopped parsley, so the parsley adheres.

10 Butter a square of greaseproof paper and spread on the remaining celery and the celeriac on it. Season well with salt and pepper. Cook in a steam-cooker for 5 minutes.

7 Bring the fish stock to a boil with the livers and parsley trimmings. Boil for 2 minutes, then remove from the heat.

11 Sear the fish fillets in hot oil, skin-side down first, then turn and sear the other side. Cook each side 2 to 3 minutes.

8 Add 2 sticks of chopped celery to the fish stock and process in a food processor. Season lightly with salt and pepper.

12 Serve the cooked celery and celeriac topped with the fillets, and the hot sauce, blended a second time. Garnish with fresh herbs (chervil).

STUFFED POUSSINS

WITH

GRAPES

SERVES : 8

PREPARATION TIME : 1 Hour 30 Minutes
COOKING TIME : 1 Hour 15 Minutes

Poussins are first boned, then stuffed with a mixture of minced turkey breast, bread, milk and herbs, then baked. They are made with a sauce made with fresh pressed grapes and chicken stock thickened with butter. Accompany with sautéed onion and courgette.

INGREDIENTS

- ☐ 2 young poussins
- ☐ 300g/12oz turkey breast
- ☐ ½ egg, beaten
- ☐ 2 shallots
- ☐ 1 tbsp chopped parsley
- ☐ 100g/4oz bread
- ☐ 50ml/2 fl oz milk
- ☐ 2 tbsps cream
- ☐ 1 carrot
- ☐ 1 onion
- ☐ ¼ stick celery
- ☐ 5 tbsps oil
- ☐ 2 tbsps Muscat wine
- ☐ 1 bouquet garni (parsley, thyme, bay leaf)
- ☐ 50g/2oz butter
- ☐ 1 onion, chopped
- ☐ 5 medium courgettes
- ☐ 200g/8oz grapes
- ☐ Fresh herbs (chervil)
- ☐ Salt and pepper

1 Bone the poussins, cutting along the breast bone to begin. Remove all the meat from the carcass. Reserve the carcasses.

2 Mix together in a food processor the turkey breast, egg, shallots and bread (presoaked in milk), and process for 1 minute. Add the cream and season with salt and pepper.

3 Chop the carrot, onion and celery quite finely.

4 Sear the carcasses in 2 tbsps oil with the above vegetables. When the ingredients are lightly coloured, deglaze with the Muscat wine.

5 Pour in ¼ litre/½ pint water, season and add the bouquet garni. Reduce over high heat for 15 minutes.

6 Spread the stuffing down the length of the poussins using a spatula.

7 Reshape the poussins and secure with string to form 2 sausage shapes. Season the skin side with salt and pepper.

8 Sear the stuffed poussins in 1 tbsp oil until lightly browned. Finish cooking in a hot oven (200°C/400°F/Mark 6) for 40 minutes, turning frequently.

9 In a large frying pan, heat 2 tbsps oil with 25g/1oz butter and sauté the onion and courgette until lightly coloured, and cooked through. Season to taste.

10 In a juice extractor, process ¾ of the grapes to obtain 200ml/8 fl oz juice. Cut the remaining grapes in half, and reserve for the sauce.

11 Strain the cooking juices from the poussins through a sieve to obtain 150ml/6 fl oz liquid. Reduce in a casserole with the grape juice, by ⅓. Mix in the remaining butter.

12 When cooked, slice the poussins and serve with the sautéed onion and courgette. Garnish with the sauce seasoned to taste, the reserved grape halves and fresh chervil.

CARAMELIZED CHICKEN WINGS

SERVES : 6

PREPARATION TIME : 30 Minutes
COOKING TIME : 50 Minutes

An economical dish full of flavour, chicken wings are oven-baked in a garlic, vinegar and honey sauce until lightly caramelized and served with fresh sautéed bean sprouts. The chicken wings are also good served with drinks.

INGREDIENTS

- ☐ 5 slices fresh ginger root
- ☐ 1 clove garlic
- ☐ 18 chicken wings
- ☐ 3 tbsps honey
- ☐ 5 tbsps soy sauce
- ☐ 2 tbsps vinegar
- ☐ 1 sprig thyme
- ☐ 2 bay leaves
- ☐ 400g/14oz fresh bean sprouts
- ☐ 1 tsp sesame oil
- ☐ 1 tsp sugar
- ☐ ½ bunch chives
- ☐ 10 mint leaves
- ☐ 1 tomato
- ☐ Salt and pepper

1 Peel the ginger and chop finely. Discard the central shoot from the garlic and chop the rest finely.

2 Trim the wing-tips off the chicken wings.

3 In a bowl, mix together the honey, 4 tbsps soy sauce, the garlic, ginger, 1 tbsp vinegar and 1 tbsp water.

4 In a saucepan of water, bring to a boil the chicken wings with the thyme and bay leaves. Remove and drain the wings.

5 Arrange the wings in an ovenproof dish, and pour over the honey-soy sauce mixture. Cook in a hot oven (200°C/400°F Gas Mark 6) for 40 minutes.

9 Add 1 tbsp soy sauce, 1 tbsp vinegar and the sugar to the bean sprouts after they have cooked. Cook for 2 minutes more, shaking the pan. Remove from heat.

6 Wash and drain the bean sprouts; dry on a tea towel.

10 Chop the chives. Cut the mint leaves into thin strips.

7 Sauté the bean sprouts in the sesame oil for 5 minutes, stirring frequently.

11 Cube only the flesh part of the tomato, discarding the seeds and juice.

8 Turn the chicken wings frequently as they cook, to ensure even caramelizing.

12 Serve the caramelized chicken wings on top of the bean sprouts; garnish with herbs (chives and mint) and the cubes of tomato.

YOGHURT MARINATED CHICKEN

SERVES : 6

PREPARATION TIME : 20 Minutes
COOKING TIME : 1 Hour 20 Minutes
MARINADE : 24 Hours

*A variation on Indian tandoori chicken.
Chicken pieces are marinated in a spicy yoghurt
mixture overnight, then slowly cooked on a grill.
They are served with saffron-flavoured rice.*

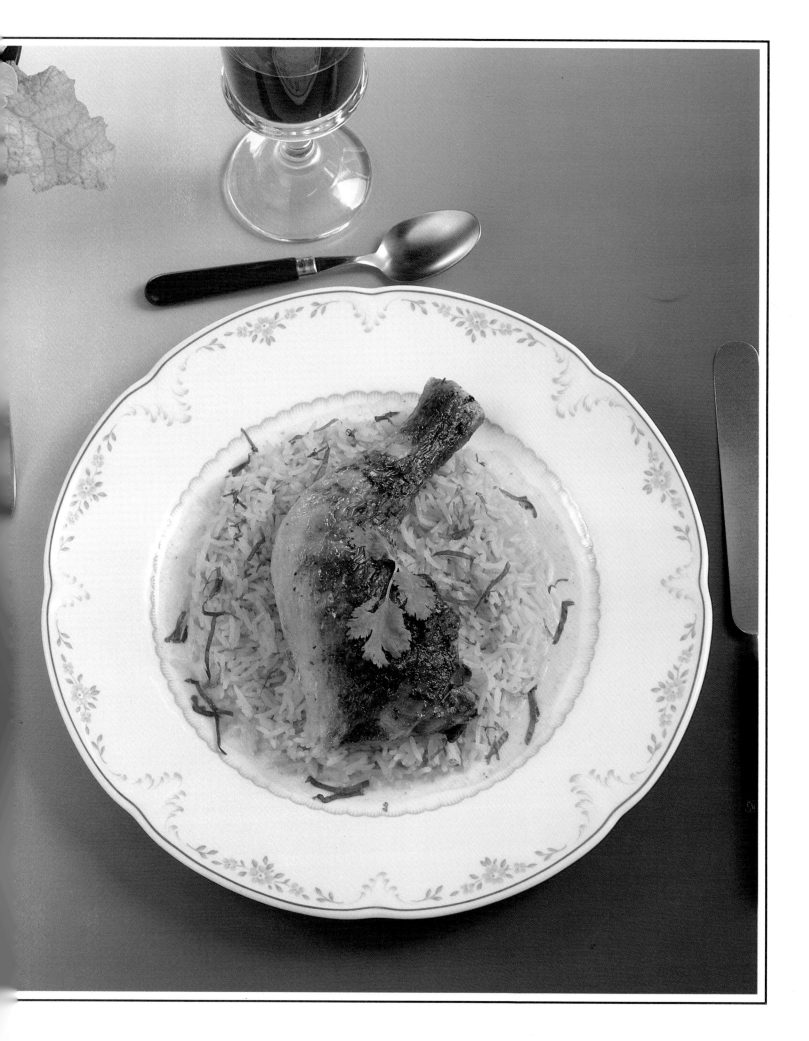

INGREDIENTS

- [ ] 1 chicken
- [ ] 2 cardamom pods
- [ ] 300ml/12oz yoghurt
- [ ] 100ml/4 fl oz milk
- [ ] 1 tsp curry powder
- [ ] 1 tsp turmeric
- [ ] ¹/₂ tsp cinnamon
- [ ] 5 tbsps olive oil
- [ ] 1 onion, chopped
- [ ] ¹/₂ small red chilli pepper
- [ ] 300g/12oz basmati rice
- [ ] 450ml/1 pint chicken stock
- [ ] A good pinch saffron
- [ ] 5 sprigs coriander
- [ ] Salt and pepper

1 Cut the chicken in half by slicing down along the backbone. Open the chicken out flat.

2 Cut away the flesh from the bones by running a sharp-bladed knife between the flesh and the bones.

3 Open up the cardamom pods, extract the seeds and chop them finely.

4 In a bowl, whisk together the yoghurt, milk and spices (curry powder, cardamon; turmeric; cinnamon), salt and pepper.

5
Place the flattened chicken in a glass baking dish, pour over the marinade and leave overnight in the refrigerator, turning frequently.

6
The next day, drain the marinade and reserve. Grill the chicken or roast in the oven, brushing it with 2 tbsps olive oil during the cooking. Turn the chicken often.

7
Heat 3 tbsps of oil and fry the onions for 1 minute. Add the chilli pepper. Add the rice to the onions. Preheat the oven to 200°C/400°F/Gas Mark 6.

8
Mix the rice and onions, then pour over the chicken stock, flavoured with the saffron. Season, cover and cook for 20 minutes in the preheated oven. Remove the chilli pepper.

9
Turn the chicken frequently during cooking. Heat the marinade in a saucepan over a low heat, stirring gently.

10
Wash, dry and finely chop the leafy part of the coriander. Set aside for the sauce.

11
When the chicken is cooked (approximately 1 hour), remove from the oven and cut into quarters.

12
Serve the chicken pieces with the hot marinade sauce, the chopped coriander and the saffron rice.

CHICKEN SUPRÊME

WITH

ASPARAGUS

SERVES : 6

PREPARATION TIME : 40 Minutes
COOKING TIME : 1 Hour

A lovely taste combination; chicken breasts are first coated in chopped fresh tarragon, then sautéed in butter and served with steamed asparagus. The delicate sauce consists of the asparagus juices enriched with cream and flavoured with tarragon.

INGREDIENTS

- ☐ 500g/1lb asparagus
- ☐ 1½ litres/3 pints chicken stock
- ☐ 1 bunch fresh tarragon
- ☐ 6 chicken breasts
- ☐ 1 egg, beaten
- ☐ 100ml/4 fl oz double cream
- ☐ 2 tbsps oil
- ☐ 15g/½oz butter
- ☐ Salt and pepper

1 Peel the asparagus with a vegetable peeler. It is not necessary to trim the tips.

2 Tie the asparagus into a neat bunch with kitchen string.

3 Stand the bunches, tips uppermost and cook in the boiling stock for 4 minutes (since the roots are tougher than the tips).

4 After 4 minutes, cook the asparagus horizontally for another 10 to 15 minutes. Remove and drain. Reserve the stock.

5 Cut off the leafy part of the tarragon. Chop finely. Add the stalks to the stock and boil for 15 minutes.

6 During this time, season the chicken breasts and brush completely with the beaten egg.

7 Coat both sides of the breasts with ¹/₂ of the chopped tarragon.

8 Cut off ¹/₃ of the asparagus stalks. Cook for an extra 10 minutes in the stock. Set aside. Cut the tips in two, lengthwise.

9 Remove the tarragon stalks from the stock. In a food processor, blend ¹/₂ litre/¹/₂ pint of the stock and the asparagus stalks smooth. Strain the sauce through a fine sieve.

10 Add almost all the remaining tarragon to the sauce. Add the cream and bring to a boil. Blend smooth again. Season.

11 Heat the oil and butter together and sear the chicken breasts on each side. Finish cooking, uncovered, in a moderate oven (180ºC/350ºF/Gas Mark 4), for 20 minutes.

12 Serve the chicken breasts and the asparagus tips with the sauce. Garnish with chopped tarragon.

TURKEY FILLET STUFFED

WITH

CHEESE

SERVES : 6

PREPARATION TIME : 50 Minutes
COOKING TIME : 35 Minutes

*An elegant yet simple preparation of turkey
breasts; thinly sliced and rolled with ham and
cheese. The dish is cooked on top of the stove or
baked in the oven. Serve with tomato halves
baked with garlic and parsley.*

INGREDIENTS

- ☐ 800g/1¾ lbs turkey breast
- ☐ 100g/4oz Gruyère or Swiss cheese
- ☐ ½ bunch chives
- ☐ 6 slices Parma ham
- ☐ 2 eggs
- ☐ 6 slices bread
- ☐ 6 tomatoes
- ☐ 1 tbsp chopped parsley
- ☐ 1 clove garlic (central shoot removed)
- ☐ 2 tbsps olive oil
- ☐ 3 tbsps oil
- ☐ 2 tbsps butter
- ☐ Fresh herbs (chervil)
- ☐ Salt and pepper

1 Cut the turkey breast into 6 long, thin escalopes.

2 Slice the cheese thinly. Chop the chives.

3 Sprinkle the chives over the cheese slices and arrange the cheese slices on the slices of ham. Roll up.

4 Cover the turkey slices with cling film and, using the flat side of a cleaver, pound them flat.

5 Place the ham and cheese rolls on the flaterred turkey slices and roll up.

6 Beat the egg, and dip the rolls in it so that they are well coated. Season with salt and pepper.

7 Process the slices of bread to form breadcrumbs.

8 Coat the turkey rolls in the breadcrumbs to cover completely.

9 Halve the tomatoes. Chop the parsley and garlic together, and place approximately 1 teaspoon on each tomato half. Sprinkle a few drops of olive oil on each.

10 Arrange the tomatoes in an ovenproof baking dish. Sprinkle over any remaining breadcrumbs. Bake in a hot oven (200ºC/400ºF/Gas Mark 6,) for 15 minutes.

11 Heat the oil and butter in a frying pan, and sear the turkey rolls on both sides. Cook over a gentle heat, for 15 to 20 minutes or bake in a moderate oven (180ºC/350ºF/Gas Mark 4).

12 Serve the turkey rolls with the tomatoes, garnished with chopped chervil.

DUCK BREAST

WITH

SPICES

SERVES : 6

PREPARATION TIME : 40 Minutes
COOKING TIME : 30 Minutes
MARINADE : 24 Hours

Duck breast is marinated for several hours or overnight in an exotic mixture of honey, soy sauce and spices. It is browned, baked and served thinly sliced with a decorative rosette of cooked tomatoes and courgettes.

INGREDIENTS

- [ ] 3 duck breasts
- [ ] 5 slices fresh ginger root, peeled
- [ ] 2 tbsps honey
- [ ] ½ tsp curry powder
- [ ] ½ tsp turmeric
- [ ] Pinch of cinnamon
- [ ] 8 tbsps soy sauce
- [ ] 3 firm tomatoes
- [ ] 1 large courgette
- [ ] 3 tbsp olive oil
- [ ] 1 sprig dried thyme
- [ ] 1 tbsp sugar
- [ ] 2 tbsps vinegar
- [ ] ½ clove garlic (central shoot removed and finely chopped)
- [ ] 6 tbsps water
- [ ] 1 tbsp chopped chives
- [ ] Salt and pepper

1 The day before, prepare the marinade. Slit the duck breasts using the point of a small knife, season on each side with salt and pepper.

2 Chop the ginger finely.

3 In a bowl, mix together the honey, curry powder turmeric, cinnamon, ginger and 3 tbsps soy sauce.

4 Brush this syrup mixture over the duck breasts and leave to marinate for 24 hours. Reserve the marinade.

5

Slice the tomatoes thinly with a serrated knife.

6

Cut the courgette into thin rounds with a sharp knife or a vegetable slicer.

7

Plunge the courgette into boiling, salted water for 1 minute. Drain and dry on a tea towel.

8

Oil squares of greaseproof paper and interlace the tomato and courgette slices to form rose shapes.

9

Season the vegetable rosettes with salt and pepper, brush lightly with olive oil and sprinkle with thyme. Before serving, cook 10 minutes in a hot oven (200°C/400°F/Gas Mark 6).

10

In a frying pan, sear the duck breasts in 2 tbsps oil, beginning skin side down and turning after 1 minute. Finish cooking in a hot oven (200°C/400°F/Gas Mark 6) for 10 to 15 minutes.

11

In a saucepan, mix together the sugar, vinegar, garlic, 5 tbsps soy sauce and 6 tbsps water. Add the reserved marinade. Bring to a boil, then remove from the heat.

12

Cut the breasts into thin slices and serve with the tomato and courgette rosettes, and a little of the warm sauce. Garnish with chopped chives.

CHICKEN POT AU FEU

WITH

SPICES

SERVES : 4

PREPARATION TIME : 45 Minutes
COOKING TIME : 1 Hour

Based on a traditional French recipe, boiled chicken is modernized with the addition of ginger, cinnamon and cloves. It is served in its stock with croutes and a home-made mayonnaise flavoured with diced gherkins and parsley.

INGREDIENTS

- ☐ 2 carrots
- ☐ 1 chicken
- ☐ 1 piece fresh ginger root, peeled
- ☐ 1 onion
- ☐ 2 whole cloves
- ☐ 1 bouquet garni (parsley, thyme, bay leaf)
- ☐ 4 cabbage leaves
- ☐ ½ leek
- ☐ ½ stick cinnamon
- ☐ 5 peppercorns
- ☐ 1 tsp coarse sea salt
- ☐ 1 egg yolk
- ☐ 1 tsp mustard
- ☐ 200ml/8 fl oz oil
- ☐ 10 gherkins
- ☐ 1 tbsp chopped parsley
- ☐ ½ French stick
- ☐ Fresh herbs (chives)
- ☐ Salt and pepper

2 Remove the legs and the breasts from the chicken. Break up the carcass.

1 Peel and cut the carrots into even-sized matchsticks. Reserve the peelings.

3 Cut 5 slices from the fresh ginger root.

4 Peel the onion, and stud it with the cloves. Tie together the parsley, thyme and bay leaf to form a bouquet garni.

5 In a casserole, cover the chicken and carcass with water. Add the carrot peelings, cabbage, leek and onion. Bring to a boil.

6 When it reaches a boil, skim off the foam. Add the ginger, cinnamon, bouquet garni, peppercorns and sea salt. Cover and cook for 45 minutes.

7 In a bowl, make a mayonnaise by mixing together the egg yolk, mustard, salt and pepper. Gradually whisk in the olive oil.

8 Chop the gherkins finely and add them to the mayonnaise along with the parsley. Mix together well and set aside.

9 When the pot-au-feu is cooked, remove the chicken and cabbage. Strain the rest through a fine sieve and return to the heat. Cook the carrot matchsticks for 6 minutes in the stock.

10 Slice the cabbage thinly, and add to the stock along with the chicken, cut into thick slices. Reheat thoroughly.

11 Toast slices of French stick under the grill, coating the slices with a little mayonnaise.

12 Serve the boiled chicken in shallow bowls with the toasts and garnished with fresh herbs (chives).

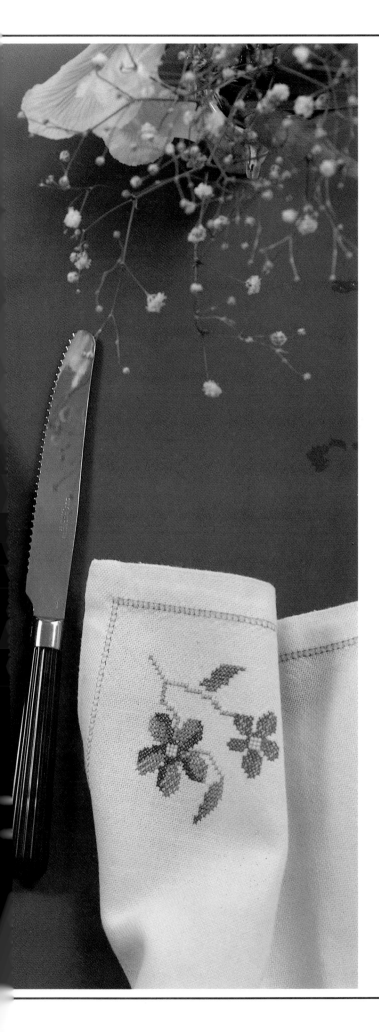

CHICKEN ROLLS STUFFED

WITH

CEPS

SERVES : 6

PREPARATION TIME : 1 Hour 30 Minutes
COOKING TIME : 1 Hour

Ceps are a wonderful, meaty wild mushroom found in speciality food shops. For this dish, they are ground with chicken breast, egg and cream and used to stuff boned chicken legs which are rolled, tied and cooked in chicken stock. Slice the rolls to serve and accompany with a galette of potatoes and a cream-enriched sauce.

INGREDIENTS

- [ ] 25g/1oz dried ceps (or other wild mushrooms)
- [ ] 6 chicken legs
- [ ] 1 chicken breast
- [ ] ½ egg, beaten
- [ ] ½ bunch chives
- [ ] 1 tbsp double cream
- [ ] 1 piece pork intestine or sausage casing
- [ ] 500g/1lb potatoes
- [ ] ½ onion, chopped
- [ ] 1 tbsp chopped parsley
- [ ] 2 slices pineapple
- [ ] 1 litre/2 pints chicken stock
- [ ] 2 tbsps oil
- [ ] 100ml/4 fl oz double cream
- [ ] Fresh herbs (chives)
- [ ] Salt and pepper

1 Reconstitute the mushrooms in cold water for 1 hour, then chop finely.

2 Bone the chicken legs by running a sharp knife down and around the bone. Discard the bones.

3 In a food processor, mix together the chicken breast, beaten egg, and the chives. Season well with salt and pepper.

4 Place the meat stuffing in a bowl and mix in half the chopped mushrooms and the 1 tbsp cream.

5 Spread the stuffing down the centres of the boned chicken legs, using a spatula.

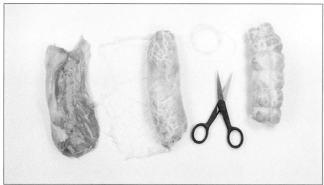

6 Roll up tightly, then place on 6 squares of pork intestine or sausage casing. Roll up and tie with string. Season.

7 Peel and rinse the potatoes. Grate them all.

8 Mix together in a bowl the potato, onion, parsley, salt and pepper. Dice the pineapple and stir it in.

9 Pour the stock into a casserole, add the chicken rolls and simmer for 30 minutes.

10 In a small frying pan, heat the oil and cook thick rounds of the potato mixture to form galettes, browning on each side. Bake in a hot oven (200°C/400°F/Gas Mark 6) 10 minutes each side.

11 Remove the chicken rolls, and cut the string. Reduce the stock by half. Using a hand-held electric mixer, incorporate the cream and remaining mushrooms.

12 Slice the chicken rolls evenly to serve. Accompany with the potato galettes, and the sauce kept warm over hot water. Garnish with chopped chives.

RABBIT STEW
À L'ANCIENNE

SERVES : 6

PREPARATION TIME : 45 Minutes
COOKING TIME : 2 Hours 10 Minutes

This is a recipe for rabbit cooked "in the old style"; a traditional stew of rabbit, bacon, onions, and potatoes. The sauce consists of a reduction of the cooking juices.

INGREDIENTS

- ☐ 1 large rabbit
- ☐ 4 cloves garlic
  (central shoots removed)
- ☐ 1 onion
- ☐ 200g/8oz bacon, in one piece
- ☐ 1 bouquet garni
  (10 sprigs parsley, thyme, bay leaf)
- ☐ 3 tbsps olive oil
- ☐ ¼ litre/½ pint red wine
- ☐ 200g/8oz small onions
- ☐ 1 tbsp sugar
- ☐ 15g/½oz butter
- ☐ 12 new potatoes
- ☐ Fresh herbs (chervil)
- ☐ Salt and pepper

2 Peel the onion and garlic. Remove the central shoot of the garlic. Chop the onion and garlic finely.

1 Chop the rabbit into 12 pieces. Discard the head and the ends of the feet.

3 Remove the bacon rind, slice and then chop the bacon into small rectangles.

4 Make a bouquet garni by tying together the parsley, thyme and bay leaf.

5 In a flameproof casserole, sear the rabbit pieces in the olive oil until lightly browned. Remove from the casserole.

6 In the same oil, fry the garlic, onion and the bouquet garni. Add the bacon pieces. Allow to colour lightly.

7 Pour off the excess fat, if necessary. Return the rabbit to the pan and deglaze with the red wine. Add ³/₄ litre/1/1¹/₂ pints water. Cover and cook over a low heat for 1 hour 45 minutes.

8 Peel the small onions, and remove the outer layers and root ends. Rinse well.

9 Cook the onions in water to cover, with the sugar, butter. Season. Cook until the water has evaporated, and the sauce is slightly caramelized (approx. 20 min).

10 Peel and trim the potatoes into narrow oblongs.

11 After the rabbit stew has been cooking for 1 hour 30 minutes, add the potatoes. Cook, covered, until tender.

12 Serve the rabbit stew with the potatoes, small onions, and garnish with chopped chervil.

CHICKEN BREASTS STUFFED

WITH

MUSHROOMS

SERVES : 6

PREPARATION TIME : 35 Minutes
COOKING TIME : 40 Minutes

Chicken breasts are stuffed with minced chicken meat, egg and finely chopped mushrooms. They are cooked and served with pleurote mushrooms and a sauce of reduced chicken stock enriched with butter. If pleurote mushrooms are not available, substitute with another variety.

INGREDIENTS

- ☐ 200g/8oz button mushrooms
- ☐ Juice $\frac{1}{2}$ lemon
- ☐ 100g/4oz butter
- ☐ 1 tbsp crème fraîche (or double cream)
- ☐ 7 chicken breasts
- ☐ 1 egg, beaten
- ☐ 3 tbsps chopped parsley
- ☐ 300g/12oz pleurote mushrooms (or other wild variety)
- ☐ 1 clove garlic (central shoot removed)
- ☐ 300ml/12 fl oz chicken stock
- ☐ Fresh herbs (chervil)
- ☐ Salt and pepper

1 Trim the stems of the button mushrooms. Wash lightly and set aside to drain.

2 Cut the mushrooms in four, then chop finely in a food processor with the lemon juice.

3 Melt 50g/2oz of the butter in a frying pan. When bubbling, add the mushrooms, sauté for 10 minutes over a high heat, stirring often.

4 Add the cream, salt and pepper to taste, and sauté for another 5 minutes. Allow to cool.

5

Process one skinned chicken breast until minced, then add ½ the beaten egg. Season well. Mix into the cooled mushroom with 1 tbsp chopped parsley.

6

Cut open the remaining breasts lengthwise, but do not cut through completely. Season.

7

Brush the insides of the opened chicken breasts with the remaining beaten egg. Fill each with some of the stuffing. Reconstruct and set aside.

8

Steam the stuffed breasts for 15 minutes.

9

Trim the stalks of the pleurote mushrooms, wash lightly, and drain thoroughly. Slice the mushrooms thinly.

10

Sauté the mushrooms in 25g/1oz of butter over medium heat. Add 1 tbsp parsley, the garlic, and salt and pepper. Cook for 10 minutes.

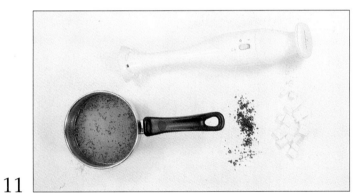

11

Reduce the stock by half, add 1 tbsp parsley, then gradually mix in 25g/1oz butter in small pieces using a hand held electric mixer.

12

Serve the stuffed chicken breasts with the pleurote mushrooms and the butter sauce. Garnish with fresh chervil.

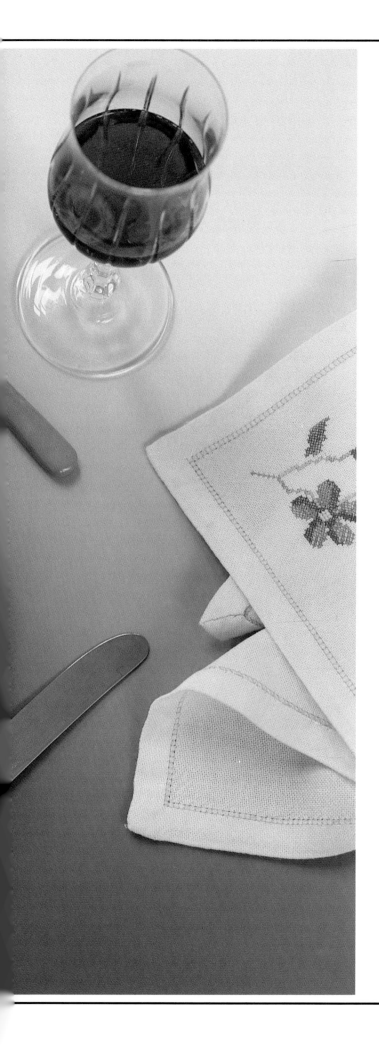

GUINEA HEN
WITH CABBAGE
PANCAKES
AND PRUNES

SERVES : 4

PREPARATION TIME : 35 Minutes
COOKING TIME : 1 Hour 20 Minutes

In this original and unusual recipe, a guinea hen is steamed in a casserole with diced root vagetables and prunes. The cooking liquid is reduced to make a sauce. The dish is served with a purée of cabbage, mixed with egg and garlic and cooked like a crepe.

INGREDIENTS

- ☐ 2 carrots
- ☐ 1 onion
- ☐ 1 bouquet garni (parsley, thyme, bay leaf)
- ☐ 1 ready-to-cook guinea hen
- ☐ 5 tbsps olive oil
- ☐ 3 tbsps butter
- ☐ 12 prunes
- ☐ ¼ litre/½ pint chicken stock
- ☐ ½ white cabbage
- ☐ 1 litre/1¾ pints milk
- ☐ 1 bunch chives
- ☐ 3 eggs
- ☐ ½ clove garlic, chopped (central shoot removed)
- ☐ Fresh herbs
- ☐ Salt and pepper

1   Dice the carrot finely. Chop the onion. Make a bouquet garni, by tying together the parsley, thyme and bay leaf.

2   Season the guinea hen and sear it on all sides in 2 tbsps of oil and half the butter, in a frying pan.

3   Remove the guinea hen. To the same pan add the carrot, onion and prunes, and sauté. Do not allow to colour too much.

4   Put back the guinea hen, pour in the stock, add the bouquet garni, cover, and cook on a low heat for 30 minutes.

5 Open the cabbage, separate the leaves, cut out the stalks, then shred the leaves finely.

6 In a large saucepan, cook the cabbage in salted milk, covered, for 40 minutes on a moderate heat.

7 Strain after cooking, then blend smooth with 50ml/2 fl oz of the cooking milk. Chop the chives.

8 Place the cabbage purée in a bowl, whisk in the eggs, chives, garlic, salt and pepper.

9 Heat the remaining oil and butter in a small frying pan. Use the cabbage mixture to make 4 pancakes.

10 Cook each one for 5 minutes on one side, turn, and cook for 4 minutes more over a low heat.

11 When the guinea hen is cooked through, remove, drain, and cut into 4. Remove the bouquet garni, and reserve the juice.

12 Serve the guinea hen portions with a little of the juice, the vegetables, prunes and the cabbage pancakes, garnished with chopped herbs (chives).

MARINATED STEAK

WITH

CORIANDER

SERVES : 6

PREPARATION TIME : 40 Minutes
COOKING TIME : 1 Hour 10 Minutes
MARINADE : 2 Hours

A quickly prepared dish of steak marinated in white wine and coriander, a spice which gives a bitter-sweet flavour. The meat is quickly fried and served with individual carrot mousses and a sauce made from the marinade, enriched with cream.

INGREDIENTS

- ☐ 1 carrot
- ☐ ½ onion
- ☐ 1 bouquet garni (parsley, thyme, bay leaf)
- ☐ 6 tender beef steaks
- ☐ 40 coriander seeds
- ☐ ¼ litre/½ pint white wine
- ☐ 450g/1lb carrots
- ☐ 2 tbsps crème fraîche (or double cream)
- ☐ 4 eggs
- ☐ ½ tsp cinnamon
- ☐ 25g/1oz butter, melted
- ☐ 150ml/6 fl oz double cream
- ☐ 2 tbsps oil
- ☐ Fresh herbs (chervil)
- ☐ Salt and pepper

1 Peel and dice the carrot and the onion. Make a bouquet garni by tying together the parsley, thyme and bay leaf.

2 Place the meat in a glass baking dish. Add 30 crushed coriander seeds, the onion, the carrot and the bouquet garni. Cover with the wine.

3 Marinate the meat for 2 hours. Peel the 450g/1lb carrots and slice into rounds.

4 Boil the sliced carrots in salted water for approximately 20 minutes.

5

Strain the cooked carrots, reserving the water. Blend smooth in a food processor, adding a little cooking water, if necessary.

6

In a bowl, whisk into the carrot purée, the crème fraîche. Beat in the eggs and cinnamon. Season with salt and pepper.

7

Brush 6 small moulds with 1 tsp melted butter.

8

Fill the moulds ¾ full with the carrot mixture. Cook in a "bain-marie" in a low oven (150°C/300°F/Gas Mark 2) for 30 to 40 minutes.

9

Remove the meat and bouquet garni from the marinade. In a saucepan, reduce the marinade by half over a high heat. Strain the reduced marinade through a fine sieve.

10

Blend the cream into the marinade with a hand-held electric mixer, adding the remaining coriander seeds. Return the vegetables to the sauce, and keep warm over hot water.

11

In a frying pan, melt the remaining butter with the oil. Dry the steaks with kitchen paper. Sear, season and cook to taste (2-10 minutes).

12

Serve the steaks sliced and spread into fan shapes, with the carrot mousses and marinade sauce. Garnish with chopped chervil.

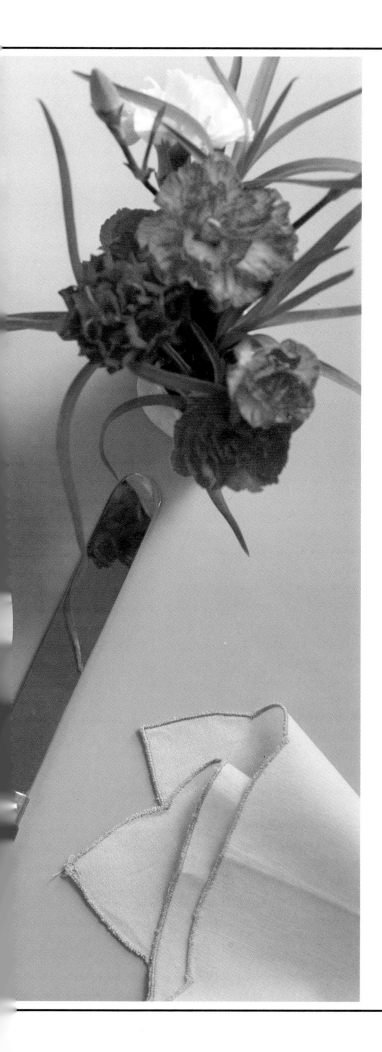

MINUTE STEAK

AND

POTATOES
AU GRATIN

SERVES : 6

PREPARATION TIME : 35 Minutes
COOKING TIME : 1 Hour 45 Minutes

An elegant meat and potato dish. Entrecote steak is cooked quickly and served with a red wine sauce and a traditional "gratin dauphinoise", sliced potato baked with butter and cream, and browned in the oven with cheese.

INGREDIENTS

- [ ] 2 shallots
- [ ] 1kg/2¼lbs potatoes
- [ ] 250ml/½ pint double cream
- [ ] 250ml/½ pint milk
- [ ] Nutmeg
- [ ] 25g/1oz butter, melted
- [ ] 1 clove garlic, chopped (central shoot removed)
- [ ] 1 tbsp chopped parsley
- [ ] 100ml/4 fl oz port
- [ ] 100ml/4 fl oz red wine
- [ ] 100ml/4 fl oz double cream
- [ ] 600g/1lb 6 oz sirloin steak
- [ ] 4 tbsps oil
- [ ] Fresh herbs (chervil)
- [ ] Salt and pepper

1 Peel and chop the shallots finely. Set aside for the sauce.

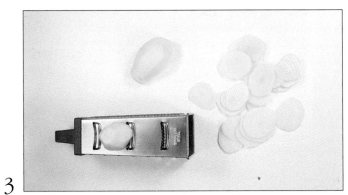

2 Peel the potatoes with a vegetable peeler. Immerse in cold water to prevent discoloration.

3 With the help of a vegetable slicer, slice the potatoes.

4 In a bowl, mix together the 250ml/½ pint cream, milk, salt, pepper and a pinch of nutmeg.

5 Brush a glass ovenproof dish with butter, and sprinkle with finely chopped garlic.

6 Alternate layers of potato and parsley in the dish.

7 Pour the cream and milk mixture over the potatoes. Cover with foil, and cook for about 1 hour 45 minutes in a moderate oven (180°C/350°F/Gas Mark 4).

8 In a saucepan, reduce the port, shallots and red wine by ³⁄₄ (approximately 10 to 15 minutes).

9 Mix in the 100ml/4 fl oz cream with a hand-held electric mixer, season to taste and keep warm over hot water.

10 Cut the steak into very thin slices with a long, sharp knife.

11 Heat a little oil in a frying pan, and fry the steaks for approximately 30 seconds each side.

12 Serve the steaks immediately with a little sauce, accompanied by the potatoes au gratin. Garnish with the chervil.

BOILED BEEF
À LA PROVENÇALE

SERVES : 6

PREPARATION TIME : 50 Minutes
COOKING TIME : 3 Hours 15 Minutes

*Several different cuts of beef are simmered
slowly with root vegetables and herbs in an old-
style way. The dish is served with croutes,
garnished with marrow, a vinaigrette sauce
and a home-made garlic mayonnaise called
"aïoli."*

INGREDIENTS

- ☐ 3 carrots
- ☐ 6 small turnips
- ☐ ¼ cabbage
- ☐ 1 leek
- ☐ 1 bouquet garni (parsley, thyme, bay leaf)
- ☐ 400g/14oz thick round steak
- ☐ 400g/14oz chuck steak
- ☐ 400g/14oz braising steak
- ☐ 2 marrow bones
- ☐ 1 onion, stuck with 2 whole cloves
- ☐ 5 peppercorns
- ☐ 1 egg yolk
- ☐ 200ml/8 fl oz olive oil
- ☐ 1 tsp mustard
- ☐ 2 cloves garlic (central shoot removed)
- ☐ 12 slices French bread
- ☐ 2 shallots, chopped
- ☐ 1 tbsp vinegar
- ☐ 2 tbsps oil
- ☐ Coarse salt
- ☐ Fresh herbs (chervil)
- ☐ Salt and pepper

1 Peel the carrots and turnips. Trim the cabbage, removing the hard core. Cut open and wash the leek. Wash the parsley.

2 Make a large bouquet garni with the cut-open leek, parsley, thyme and bay leaf. Tie together securely with string and set aside.

3 Place the meat and bones in a large pan and cover with water. Bring to a boil and skim the foam off the top, as necessary.

4 Add the whole turnips, carrots, clove-studded onion, bouquet garni, peppercorns and salt. Remove the marrow bones after 10 minutes. Simmer the rest, covered, for 3 hours.

5

Shake the marrow from the bones. Allow to cool. For the mayonnaise, whisk together the egg yolks, mustard, salt and pepper.

9

When the meat is cooked, remove and cut into even slices.

6

Whisk in the oil, drop by drop. When thick, add the finely chopped garlic and mix well.

10

Remove the vegetables and cut into neat shapes.

7

Slice the bread into attractive shapes and grill on both sides.

11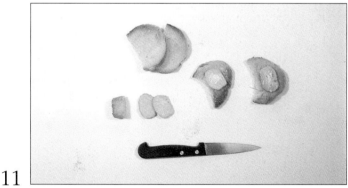

Cut the cold marrow, place on the bread croutes, then sprinkle over a little coarse salt. Heat in a moderate oven just before serving.

8

Make a vinaigrette dressing by mixing together the shallots, salt, pepper, vinegar and olive oil. Set aside.

12

Serve the sliced meat with the vegetables, accompanied with the mayonnaise, vinaigrette dressing and marrow croutes. Sprinkle with fresh chervil.

STEAK WITH RED WINE SAUCE AND GREEN PEPPERCORNS

SERVES : 6

PREPARATION TIME : 45 Minutes
COOKING TIME : 45 Minutes

This is an easy-to-prepare dish of fried steak with a red wine and mushroom sauce spiced with green peppercorns. It is served with sautéed fresh artichoke hearts.

INGREDIENTS

- ☐ 6 globe artichokes
- ☐ 1 lemon (juice and peel)
- ☐ 150g/6oz mushrooms
- ☐ 2 shallots, chopped
- ☐ 4 sprigs parsley
- ☐ 10 green peppercorns
- ☐ ½ litre/1 pint red wine
- ☐ 200ml/8 fl oz double cream
- ☐ 1kg/2lbs tender beef steak
- ☐ Mixed peppercorns, in a grinder
- ☐ 2 tbsps oil
- ☐ 50g/2oz butter
- ☐ Fresh herbs (chervil)
- ☐ Salt and pepper

1 Use medium-sized artichokes. Remove the artichoke stems.

2 Trim away all the leaves, without cutting too deeply into the artichoke heart. Cut away the "choke", leaving the hearts.

3 Sprinkle the artichoke hearts with lemon juice to prevent discoloration. Add the lemon peel to a large quantity of water and boil the artichoke hearts for 20 minutes.

4 Trim the stumps off the mushrooms. Wash lightly and drain thoroughly. Slice finely.

5 Finely chop the shallots and parsley, which has been washed and well dried.

9 Cut the beef into 6 pieces, season with salt and freshly ground mixed peppercorns.

6 Place the shallots, green peppercorns, red wine and mushrooms in a saucepan. Bring to a boil and cook until reduced by ³/₄. Set aside.

10 In a frying pan, melt 40g/1¹/₂oz of the butter with the oil, and cook the steaks to taste. Heat the remaining butter in a separate frying pan.

7 When the artichoke hearts are cooked, cool in cold water. Remove the remaining "bearded" centre with a spoon, then cube.

11 Sauté the artichoke hearts, sprinkle over the parsley, and season to taste. Serve the steaks with the red wine sauce and the artichoke hearts.

8 Add the cream to the reduced sauce, mix well and reheat gently. Season to taste, then whisk well.

12 Garnish with a few freshly chopped herbs.

BRAISED BEEF

WITH

CARAMELIZED

CARROTS

SERVES : 6

PREPARATION TIME : 30 Minutes
COOKING TIME : 2 Hours 30 Minutes

A relatively economical main course, braising beef is slowly cooked with bacon, small onions and aromatic herbs and served with lightly caramelized sautéed carrots to add a slightly sweet taste.

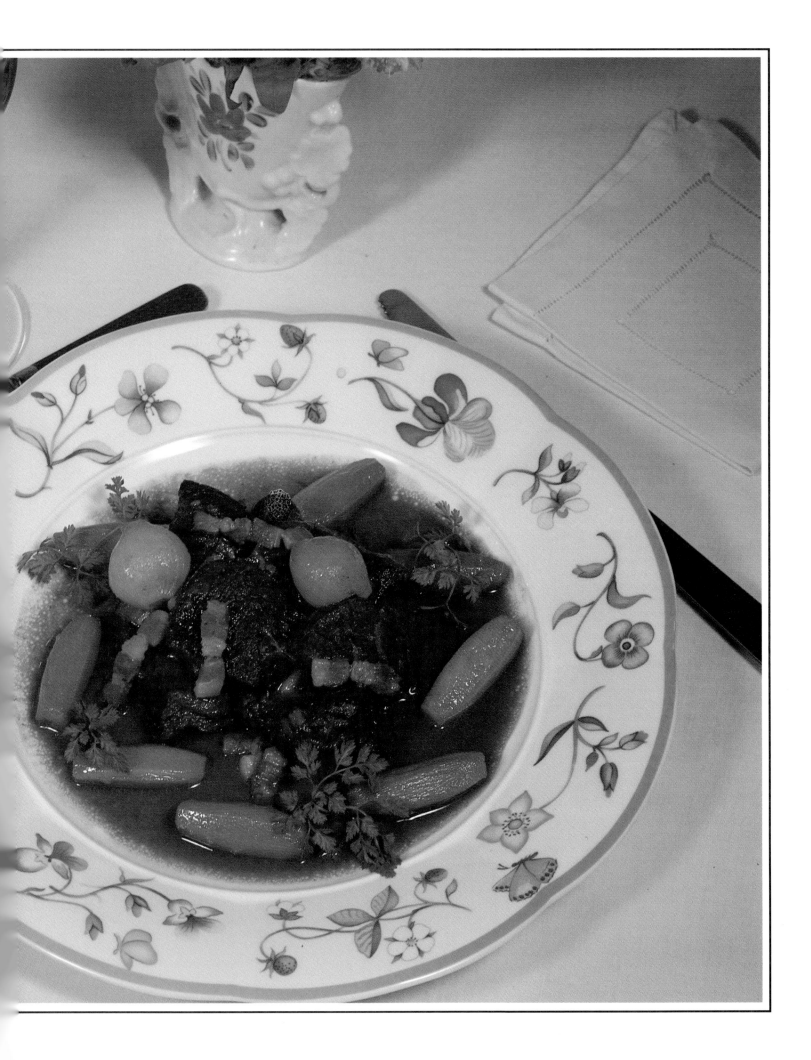

INGREDIENTS

- ☐ 1.2 kg/2½lbs braising steak
- ☐ 1 onion
- ☐ ½ stick celery
- ☐ 800g/2lbs carrots
- ☐ 200g/8oz small onions
- ☐ 150g/6oz smoked bacon (in one piece)
- ☐ 3 tbsps olive oil
- ☐ ½ litre/1 pint red wine
- ☐ 3 cloves garlic (central shoot removed)
- ☐ Bouquet garni (parsley, thyme, bay leaf)
- ☐ 5 tsps sugar
- ☐ Fresh herbs (chervil)
- ☐ Salt and pepper

1 Cut the meat into thick slices, then into large, even-sized cubes.

2 Chop the onion and the celery finely.

3 Peel the carrots, cut them into chunks, slice in two lengthwise, then trim into long, oval shapes. (Keep the trimmings.)

4 Soak the small onions for 1 minute in warm water, and peel with a small, sharp knife (soaking facilitates peeling.).

5 Cut off the bacon rind and cut the bacon first into slices and then into small pieces.

6 Heat the oil and sear the meat on each side, browning lightly (approximately 2 minutes).

7 Add the celery, onion and carrot trimmings to the meat. Fry for 1 minute.

8 Pour over the wine, add the garlic, bouquet garni, salt and pepper, and ¹/₂ litre/1 pint water. Cover and simmer for 2¹/₂ hours.

9 Cook the carrots in boiling salted water for 8 minutes. Drain and rinse.

10 Glaze the carrots in a frying pan with the sugar and 5 tbsps of water on a gentle heat, shaking the pan continuously until the liquid has evaporated.

11 Remove the meat with a fork, place in another casserole, strain the stock over the beef and add the onions and the bacon. Cook for 20 minutes more.

12 Serve the braised beef, onions and glazed carrots garnished with fresh, chopped herbs.

PORK FILLET

WITH

MUSTARD SAUCE

SERVES : 6

PREPARATION TIME : 35 Minutes
COOKING TIME : 1 Hour 10 Minutes

A classic flavour combination. Roast fillet of pork is stuffed with garlic and prunes and served with a grain mustard sauce accompanied with shredded white cabbage sautéed with bacon.

INGREDIENTS

- ☐ 1 large pork fillet (1½kg/2½lbs)
- ☐ 8 prunes
- ☐ 1 tsp chopped garlic, (central shoot removed)
- ☐ 4 tbsps olive oil
- ☐ 2 spring cabbages
- ☐ 200g/8oz bacon
- ☐ 25g/1oz butter
- ☐ 50ml/2 fl oz white wine
- ☐ 100ml/4 fl oz chicken stock
- ☐ 150ml/6 fl oz double cream
- ☐ 2 tbsps mustard
- ☐ Fresh herbs (chervil)
- ☐ Salt and pepper

1 Cut open the pork fillet lengthwise, but do not cut all the way through. Stone the prunes.

2 Season the meat all over, spread the prunes and the garlic down the centre of the fillet.

3 Roll up and close the fillet. Secure well with kitchen string.

4 In 4 tbsps of oil, sear and brown the meat on all sides, then transfer to a hot oven (200°C/400°F/Gas Mark 6) for 40 minutes.

5

Remove the outer cabbage leaves and discard. Separate the leaves, wash and slice finely.

9

Add to the bacon the well-drained cabbage. Season, mix well, and cook gently for 20 minutes, stirring occasionally.

6

Blanch for 3 minutes in boiling, salted water, then plunge in cold water. Set aside to drain.

10

When cooked, remove the pork from the oven, pour off any excess fat, and deglaze with the wine. Stir and pour into a saucepan; reduce the sauce for 5 minutes. Add the cream.

7

Remove the bacon rind, and cut the bacon into small pieces.

11

Add the mustard, and blend with a hand-held electric mixer. Heat through, but do not boil. Slice the meat.

8

In the butter, fry the bacon quickly to brown it lightly.

12

Serve the pork in slices, accompanied with the cabbage and sauce. Garnish with fresh, chopped chervil.

CARAMELIZED PORK SPARERIBS

WITH

LEMON GRASS

SERVES : 6

PREPARATION TIME : 1 Hour 30 Minutes
COOKING TIME : 40 Minutes

This is an Oriental-inspired dish of pork spareribs baked in the oven with soy sauce, honey and lemon grass until lightly caramelized. The sweet and savoury taste is emphasized with a side dish of puréed sweet potatoes.

INGREDIENTS

- ☐ 1.2kg/2¹⁄₂lbs pork spareribs
- ☐ 1 carrot
- ☐ 1 onion
- ☐ 1 bouquet garni (parsley, thyme, bay leaf)
- ☐ 1 stalk lemon grass
- ☐ 2 tbsps honey
- ☐ 1 tbsp wine vinegar
- ☐ 3 tbsps soy sauce
- ☐ 1 clove garlic (central shoot removed)
- ☐ 5 slices ginger root, peeled and chopped
- ☐ 800g/2lbs sweet potatoes
- ☐ 1 tbsp olive oil
- ☐ 1 onion, chopped
- ☐ 2 tbsps double cream
- ☐ 100ml/4 fl oz milk
- ☐ Fresh herbs (chives)
- ☐ Salt and pepper

1 Separate the spareribs, cutting between the bones. Cut the bone in half lengthwise, if too long.

2 Peel and slice the onion and carrot.

3 In a flameproof casserole, cover the spareribs, onion, carrot and bouquet garni with water. Bring to a boil.

4 After allowing the spareribs to boil for 1 minute, remove and drain together with the onion, carrot and bouquet garni. Place the ribs in a glass baking dish.

5 Slice the lemon grass thinly lengthwise. Then chop finely.

6 In a bowl, whisk together the honey, vinegar, soy sauce, lemon grass, garlic and the ginger. Stir in 1 tbsp water.

7 Pour this mixture over the spareribs, mix together well, and cook for approximately 40 minutes in a hot oven (200°C/ 400°F/Gas Mark 6).

8 Peel the sweet potatoes with a vegetable peeler, and cut into small, even-sized pieces.

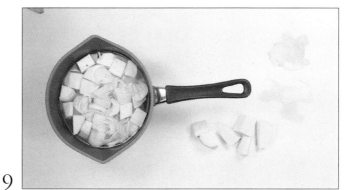

9 Simmer the sweet potatoes for 35 minutes in a large quantity of salted water with the chopped onion and 1 tbsp olive oil.

10 As the ribs are baking, remove them frequently from the oven and stir them with a wooden spatula.

11 Drain the sweet potatoes when cooked, and mash to a purée. Stir in the milk and cream. Season to taste, and keep warm over hot water.

12 Remove the caramelized spare ribs from the oven, and arrange over a bed of sweet potato purée. Garnish with the chives.

LAMB STEW
À LA
PROVENÇALE

SERVES : 6

PREPARATION TIME : 1 Hour 30 Minutes
COOKING TIME : 1 Hour 30 Minutes

*Boneless lamb shoulder meat is slowly stewed
with garlic and basil for full flavour. the
Mediterranean style vegetable accompaniment
is a gratin of aubergine and tomato which goes
wonderfully with the lamb.*

INGREDIENTS

- ☐ 2kg/4½lb lamb shoulder
- ☐ 30 leaves fresh basil
- ☐ 3 cloves garlic (central shoot removed)
- ☐ 1 onion
- ☐ 3 tbsps olive oil
- ☐ 100ml/4 fl oz white wine
- ☐ 1 bouquet garni (parsley, thyme, bay leaf)
- ☐ 1 large aubergine
- ☐ 3 tomatoes
- ☐ Flour for coating
- ☐ 200ml/8 fl oz olive oil
- ☐ 100g/4oz grated cheese (Cheddar or Gruyère)
- ☐ Extra chopped fresh basil
- ☐ Salt and pepper

1 Using a sharp knife, cut all around the lamb shoulder bone to remove from the meat.

2 Trim away any substantial amounts of fat. Cut the meat into even-sized cubes.

3 Remove the leaves of basil from the stalks. Reserve these and chop the leaves finely. Chop the garlic finely. Chop the onion finely.

4 Heat 3 tbsps oil in a frying pan, and sear the meat on all sides over a high heat until the meat is lightly browned.

5 Pour off the excess fat, and add the chopped onion, garlic and basil leaves. Sauté for 1 minute.

9 Sauté the aubergine slices a few at a time in the remaining oil. Drain on kitchen paper.

6 Deglaze the pan with the white wine. Reduce until almost evaporated, add ¼ litre/½ pint water and the bouquet garni. Season. Add the basil stalks and cook, covered, for 1 hour.

10 Interlace the aubergine and tomato slices in the bottom of an ovenproof dish. Season again.

7 Slice the aubergine and tomato into rounds.

11 When the dish is full, sprinkle over the grated cheese, and bake for 25 minutes in a hot oven, (200°C/400°F/Gas Mark 6).

8 Season the aubergine slices, and coat each side with flour.

12 Serve the lamb stew with the aubergine and tomato gratin. Garnish with extra chopped basil.

LAMB NOISETTES

WITH

CAULIFLOWER

SERVES : 6

PREPARATION TIME : 1 Hour
COOKING TIME : 1 Hour 10 Minutes

*A gastronomic preparation of saddle of lamb
that is rolled with ham and seared before
baking. It is served with a sauce of puréed
cauliflower and a delicate side dish of braised
lettuce.*

INGREDIENTS

- ☐ 1 saddle of lamb (approximately 2kg/4½lbs)
- ☐ 9 very thin slices parma ham
- ☐ ¼ cauliflower
- ☐ ½ litre/1 pint milk
- ☐ 3 lettuces
- ☐ 65g/2½oz butter, melted
- ☐ 50ml/2 fl oz double cream
- ☐ Nutmeg
- ☐ 3 tbsps oil
- ☐ 10 black olives
- ☐ Fresh herbs (chervil)
- ☐ Salt and pepper

1 Bone the saddle of lamb, cut off any excess fat and gristle. Cut the meat into small medallions.

2 Cut the parma ham into strips, lengthwise. Roll around each medallion and secure neatly with kitchen string.

3 Break the cauliflower into small pieces, discarding any hard stumps.

4 Cook the cauliflower in the milk, seasoned with salt and pepper, for 30 minutes.

5 Remove and discard the outer leaves of the lettuces. Cut each one in two.

6 Plunge the two halves of lettuce into boiling salted water for 3 minutes. Repeat with all the lettuce halves (drain the lettuce and refresh in cold water).

7 Squeeze the excess water from the lettuces. Shape and place them in a buttered, ovenproof dish and bake for 30 minutes in a hot oven (200°C/400°F/Gas Mark 6) with 4 tbsps water.

8 Blend the cauliflower, cooking milk and cream in a food processor until smooth. Pour into a pan and season with salt, pepper and nutmeg.

9 Heat the oil and the remaining butter in a pan and sear the lamb medallions on each side. Transfer to a hot oven (200°C/400°F/Gas Mark 6) and cook for 8 to 15 minutes.

10 Stone the olives and chop them finely.

11 Remove the cooked lettuces from the oven and cut and shape into fans using a sharp knife.

12 Cut off the string from the meat. Serve decoratively with the lettuces. Accompany with the reheated cauliflower sauce, garnished with the chopped olives and fresh chervil.

VEAL BLANQUETTE

WITH

ROQUEFORT

SERVES : 6

PREPARATION TIME : 25 Minutes
COOKING TIME : 2 Hours

∽∾ ∾∽

This classic French veal stew in a creamy white sauce is modernized with the addition of blue cheese. The pungently flavoured blanquette is served with a simple rice pilaf.

INGREDIENTS

- ☐ 1kg/2lbs veal shoulder
- ☐ 1 leek
- ☐ 2 carrots
- ☐ 1 bouquet garni (parsley, thyme bay leaf)
- ☐ 200g/8oz mushrooms
- ☐ 1 onion, chopped
- ☐ 75g/3oz butter
- ☐ 300g/12oz rice
- ☐ 1 tbsp flour
- ☐ 150g/6oz Roquefort, crumbled
- ☐ 200ml/8oz double cream
- ☐ 1/2 bunch chives, chopped
- ☐ 1 tbsp chopped parsley
- ☐ Salt and pepper

1 Cut the meat into even-sized pieces, without removing the excess fat (the fat enhances the flavour of the dish).

2 In a flameproof casserole, cover the meat with water, bring to a boil, cook for 4 minutes, skimming the surface of the water from time to time. Remove the meat and discard the water.

3 Wash, peel and chop the leek and carrots finely.

4 In a flameproof casserole, melt 25g/1oz of the butter, sauté the leek, carrot and bouquet garni. Add the meat and cover with water. Season with salt and simmer, covered, for 1¼ hours.

5 Strain the mixture through a fine sieve, reserving the meat and stock.

6 Remove the stalks of the mushrooms, wash and chop the caps finely.

7 In an ovenproof casserole, sauté the chopped onion and mushrooms in 25g/1oz butter for 2 minutes. Preheat the oven (220°C/425°F/Gas Mark 7).

8 Add the rice and cook, stirring constantly, over a low heat for 2 minutes. Add 650ml/1¼ pints of the cooking stock. Season. Cook, covered, in the preheated oven, for 20 minutes.

9 In a saucepan, melt 25g/1oz butter, stir in the flour and cook for 1 minute over a low heat. Add 200ml/8 fl oz of the cooking stock, stir and allow to thicken for 2 minutes.

10 Add the Roquefort and the cream. Blend with a hand-held electric mixer. Season if necessary.

11 Add the meat to the sauce and reheat over a low heat for approximately 5 minutes.

12 Serve the veal blanquette with the rice, garnished with the chopped chives and parsley.

VEAL KIDNEYS

WITH

CREAMED SPINACH

SERVES : 6

PREPARATION TIME : 20 Minutes
COOKING TIME : 35 Minutes

Veal kidneys retain their tenderness when baked "en papillote" or in little foil packets. The dish is served with creamed, puréed spinach and accompanied by crisp, deep-fried straw potatoes.

INGREDIENTS

- ☐ 3 veal kidneys
- ☐ 3 tsps Cognac
- ☐ 400g/14oz spinach
- ☐ 500g/1lb good quality potatoes
- ☐ Oil for deep-frying
- ☐ 300ml/12 fl oz double cream
- ☐ Fresh herbs (chervil)
- ☐ Salt and pepper

1 Devein and cut out any fat from the kidneys. Using the tip of a sharp, small knife remove all the white parts.

2 Arrange the 3 kidneys on 3 sheets of foil, season with salt and pepper, and sprinkle with the Cognac.

3 Fold up the foil to form sealed packets. Set aside until ready to cook.

4 Trim the stalks from the spinach, and wash thoroughly.

5 Plunge the spinach in boiling, salted water, and cook for 5 minutes.

6 Drain and rinse the spinach; squeeze out the excess water. Chop as finely as possible.

7 Peel the potatoes and cut into matchsticks. Rinse well, then dry on a tea towel.

8 In a large, deep frying pan, preheat the oil and fry the potatoes in several batches.

9 When lightly browned, drain the potatoes on kitchen paper. Cook the kidneys in a hot oven (200°C/400°F/Gas Mark 6) for 8 to 15 minutes.

10 Place the chopped spinach and the cream in a flameproof casserole. Heat through gently, season, and blend with a hand held electric mixer.

11 Remove the kidneys from the oven, but allow them to rest in the foil for 5 minutes. Remove and slice.

12 Serve the sliced kidneys arranged in rounds, surrounded by the creamed spinach, with the straw potatoes in the centre. Sprinkle with fresh chervil.

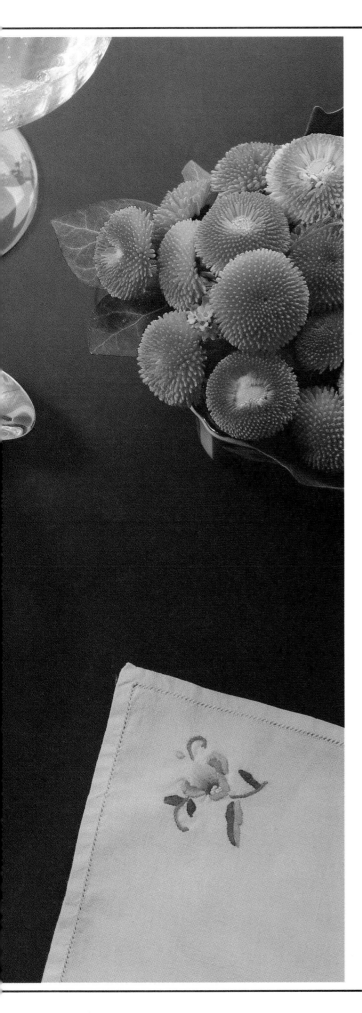

EXOTIC FRUIT SOUP

WITH

COCONUT

SERVES : 6

PREPARATION TIME : 40 Minutes

A refreshing dessert, the fruits can be varied according to season and availability. Serve in soup bowls with vanilla or coconut ice cream and all the natural juices from the fruit.

INGREDIENTS

- ☐ 1 mango
- ☐ 1 papaya
- ☐ 1 banana
- ☐ 1 kiwi fruit
- ☐ 1 small pineapple
- ☐ 12 rambutans or lychees
- ☐ 2 oranges
- ☐ 2 grapefruit
- ☐ 1 tbsp coconut liqueur
- ☐ Sugar (optional)
- ☐ ½ litre/1 pint coconut ice cream
- ☐ 1 tbsp grated coconut
- ☐ Mint leaves

1 Peel the mango with a small sharp knife, taking care not to remove too much of the flesh.

2 Cut the mango into slices, right down to the stone.

3 Cut the papaya in half, peel and remove the pips from the centre.

4 Cut the papaya halves into thin, crosswise slices.

5

Peel the banana and kiwi fruit and slice into rounds.

9

Squeeze the juice from the oranges and the grapefruit. Add the coconut liqueur.

6

With a sharp knife, cut the peel off the pineapple.

10

Mix together all the fruit with the juices and liqueur, and sweeten if necessary. Chill in the refrigerator.

7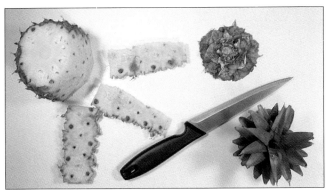

Cut out the pineapple "eyes" with the tip of a vegetable peeler. Cut the flesh into even-sized chunks.

11

Just before serving, scoop out balls of ice cream and roll them in the grated coconut.

8

Peel the rambutans or lychees, pull open the fruit and remove the stones. If this is too difficult, leave the stones in place.

12

Serve the fruit soup immediately, garnished with chopped or snipped mint.

PEAR AND HONEY CRUMBLE

SERVES : 6

PREPARATION TIME : 30 Minutes
COOKING TIME : 35 Minutes

*A French chef's version of a classic crumble,
pears are sautéed in honey and butter with the
addition of raisins and sautéed rhubarb. The
fruits are layered and topped with a delicate
crumble and baked in the oven.*

INGREDIENTS

- ☐ 6 pears (or apples)
- ☐ 40g/1½oz butter
- ☐ 50g/2oz currants
- ☐ 3 tbsps liquid honey
- ☐ 200g/8oz flour
- ☐ 100g/4oz butter
- ☐ 50g/2oz ground almonds
- ☐ 50g/2oz sugar
- ☐ 200g/8oz rhubarb
- ☐ 25g/1oz butter
- ☐ 25g/1oz sugar
- ☐ 100ml/4 fl oz double cream
- ☐ 1 tbsp cocoa powder

1 Peel the pears with a vegetable peeler. Remove the core with a melon baller.

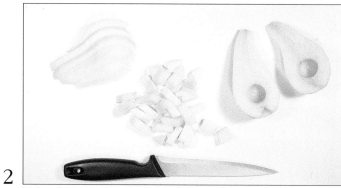

2 Halve the pears lengthwise and then cube.

3 Heat 40g/1½oz butter until hot and sauté the pear cubes.

4 When golden brown, add the currants and honey, mix well and remove from the heat.

5

Turn the pear mixture into a glass baking dish and allow to cool.

9

Sauté the rhubarb in the remaining 25g/1oz butter, add remaining sugar and cook for 3 minutes more.

6

To make the crumble, rub the 100g/4oz butter into the flour with the ground almonds.

10

Spread the cooled rhubarb mixture over the pear mixture.

7

Work in the 50g/2oz sugar, to obtain a coarse, crumbly mixture.

11

Sprinkle the crumble over to cover the fruit completely. Cook in a hot oven (200°C/400°F/Gas Mark 6) for 25 minutes.

8

Peel the rhubarb with a vegetable peeler, then cut into small chunks.

12

Serve the crumble warm with the cream (lightly sweetened, if desired), sprinkled with cocoa powder.

CHOCOLATE GANACHE

SERVES : 6

PREPARATION TIME : 1 Hour
COOKING TIME : 5 Minutes
CHILLING TIME : 6 Hours

A rich chocolate terrine consisting of layers of boudoir biscuits, a dark chocolate mousse and raspberry jam. The ganache is garnished with fresh orange slices to add a little tartness.

INGREDIENTS

- ☐ 300g/12oz plain chocolate
- ☐ 100g/4 fl oz double cream
- ☐ 25/1oz butter
- ☐ 50g/2oz egg white
- ☐ Pinch salt
- ☐ 1 sachet powdered gelatine
- ☐ 5 tbsps honey
- ☐ 20 boudoir biscuits
- ☐ 2 tbsps raspberry liqueur
- ☐ 2 tbsps water
- ☐ 100g/4oz raspberry jam
- ☐ 2 oranges

1   Cut the chocolate into fine shreds with a long, heavy knife.

2   Place the chocolate in a bowl, pour over the cream, heated to boiling point, and whisk well.

3   Add the slightly softened butter to the above and whisk well.

4   Whisk the egg whites with a pinch of salt until stiff but not dry. Soak the gelatine in a little water. Bring the honey to a boil.

5 Remove the honey from the heat and stir in the softened gelatine. Gradually pour this over the egg whites, whisking continuously to form a meringue.

6 Fold the meringue carefully into the chocolate ganache, using a spatula.

7 Cut greaseproof paper to fit a loaf tin, overhanging the sides. Place a layer of biscuits in the base. Pour over 1/2 of the ganache.

8 Mix the liqueur with 2 tbsps water and brush this over the remaining biscuits. Layer these over the ganache.

9 Spoon the jam over the biscuit layer. The jam should not be thick, but heat if necessary.

10 Pour over the remaining ganache. Pull the overhanging paper to cover the top neatly and freeze for 6 hours.

11 Peel the oranges down to the flesh. Cut into segments to serve with the chilled chocolate ganache.

12 Before serving, unmould the ganache, remove the paper and cut into slices. Dip the knife into boiling water before cutting each slice.

SWEET
SABLÉ BISCUITS
WITH
FRUIT

SERVES : 6

PREPARATION TIME : 40 Minutes
COOKING TIME : 25 Minutes

*Sablés, meaning sandy, are buttery shortcakes.
They are served with pastry cream, fresh fruit
and a custard sauce. Be creative in the last-
minute assembling and preparation of this
multi-ingredient dessert.*

INGREDIENTS

- ☐ 300g/12oz flour, sifted
- ☐ 110g/4¹/₂oz sugar
- ☐ Pinch salt
- ☐ 1 egg
- ☐ 150g/6oz butter
- ☐ 5 egg yolks
- ☐ 120g/5oz sugar
- ☐ 1 vanilla pod
- ☐ ¹/₂ litre/1 pint milk
- ☐ 2 oranges
- ☐ 2 kiwi fruit
- ☐ 1 banana
- ☐ 30 raspberries
- ☐ 200ml/8 fl oz double cream
- ☐ 25g/1oz sugar
- ☐ 4 tsps cocoa powder
- ☐ Fresh mint

1 Make the pastry by mixing together the flour, 110g/4¹/₂oz sugar, salt and egg. Rub in with your fingers to obtain a fine, crumbly mixture.

2 Add the butter, cut into small pieces. Rub in to make a firm dough. Form into a ball, flour lightly and chill.

3 Make a soft custard by mixing together the egg yolks and 125g/5oz sugar. Cut the vanilla pod in half, extract the seeds and add the seeds to the above.

4 Bring the milk to a boil and add it slowly to the egg and sugar. Pour back into the pan and place over a gentle heat.

5 Cook, stirring constantly, for 7 to 10 minutes, until thickened. Cool and then chill.

9 Place on a nonstick baking sheet and cook in a hot oven (200ºC/400ºF/Gas Mark 6) for 10 to 15 minutes. Allow to cool on the baking sheet.

6 Prepare the fruit. Separate the oranges into segments, cut the kiwi fruit and banana into rounds. Leave the raspberries whole.

10 Place the cream in a bowl, freeze for 5 minutes then whip until slightly thickened.

7 Remove the pastry from the refrigerator 10 minutes before rolling. Roll out thinly with a floured rolling pin on a floured surface.

11 As the cream begins to thicken add the sugar and continue whipping until thick.

8 Cut out 12 medium-sized rounds with a pastry cutter.

12 Assemble all the ingredients; the biscuit bases, custard, fruit and whipped cream. Arrange together as you like, and decorate with the sieved cocoa powder.

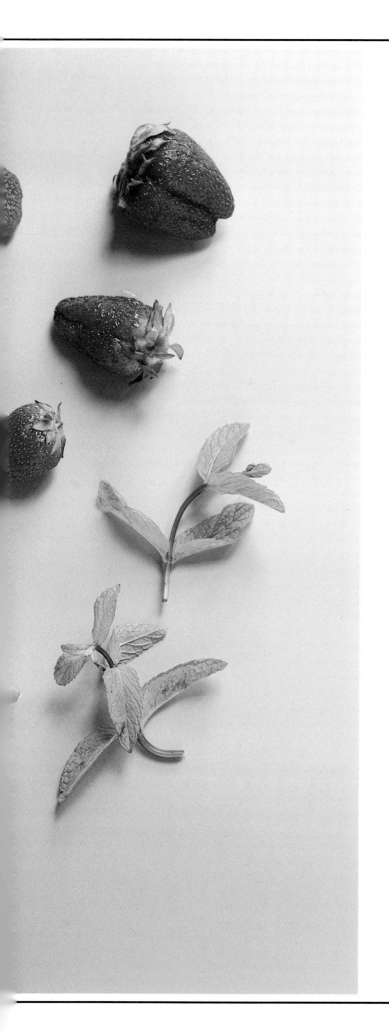

ORANGE MERINGUE TART

SERVES : 6

PREPARATION TIME : 35 Minutes
COOKING TIME : 40 Minutes

*Here is a variaton on the classic lemon
meringue pie. Fresh orange juice and orange
peel are essential for flavouring the filling. The
tart is topped with meringue, and caramelized
in the oven. Serve with fresh soft fruits, if in
season.*

INGREDIENTS

- ☐ 200g/8oz flour
- ☐ 25g/1oz sugar
- ☐ 3 tbsps water
- ☐ 1 egg yolk
- ☐ 100g/4oz butter
- ☐ 2 oranges
- ☐ 6 eggs
- ☐ 140g/6oz sugar
- ☐ 120g/5oz butter
- ☐ 100g/4oz dried beans
- ☐ 3 egg whites
- ☐ 3 tbsps icing sugar
- ☐ Pinch salt

1 Make the pastry. Pile the flour on your work surface or in a bowl. Make a well in the centre and place the 25g/1oz sugar, salt, water and egg yolk in it.

2 Rub in the ingredients with your fingers to mix well. Add the 100g/4oz butter at room temperature, cut into small pieces.

3 Mix in the butter to form a ball of dough. Sprinkle with flour and allow to rest in the refrigerator.

4 Cut off the zest of ¹/₂ orange with a vegetable peeler. Squeeze the juice from the 2 oranges.

5 Cut the zest into thin strips. Place in a saucepan of water, bring to a boil, strain and rinse. Set aside to drain.

9 Roll the pastry to fit into a flan dish. Prick with a fork. Cover with paper, top with the beans and cook in the preheated oven for 25 minutes. Remove paper and beans and cool.

6 In a saucepan, whisk together the orange juice, eggs, sugar, 120g/5oz butter and orange zest.

10 Whisk the egg whites together with a pinch of salt and ½ the icing sugar. After 1 minute add the remaining sugar, whisk until stiff.

7 Whisk continuously over a gentle heat for about 10 minutes. The mixture will gradually thicken.

11 Spread the warm orange filling over the cooked, cooled pastry case. Pipe the meringue decoratively over the filling.

8 Take out the pastry 10 minutes before rolling. Roll out on a floured surface. Preheat the oven (200°C/400°F/Gas Mark 6).

12 Brown the meringue lightly under a hot grill. Serve when cool.

SPICE CAKE

SERVES : 6

PREPARATION TIME : 30 Minutes
COOKING TIME : 50 Minutes

*This sweet spice cake is based on a traditional
"quatre-quarts" cake which is the French
equivalent of our well-known Pound Cake. It is
served with a cinnamon custard sauce.*

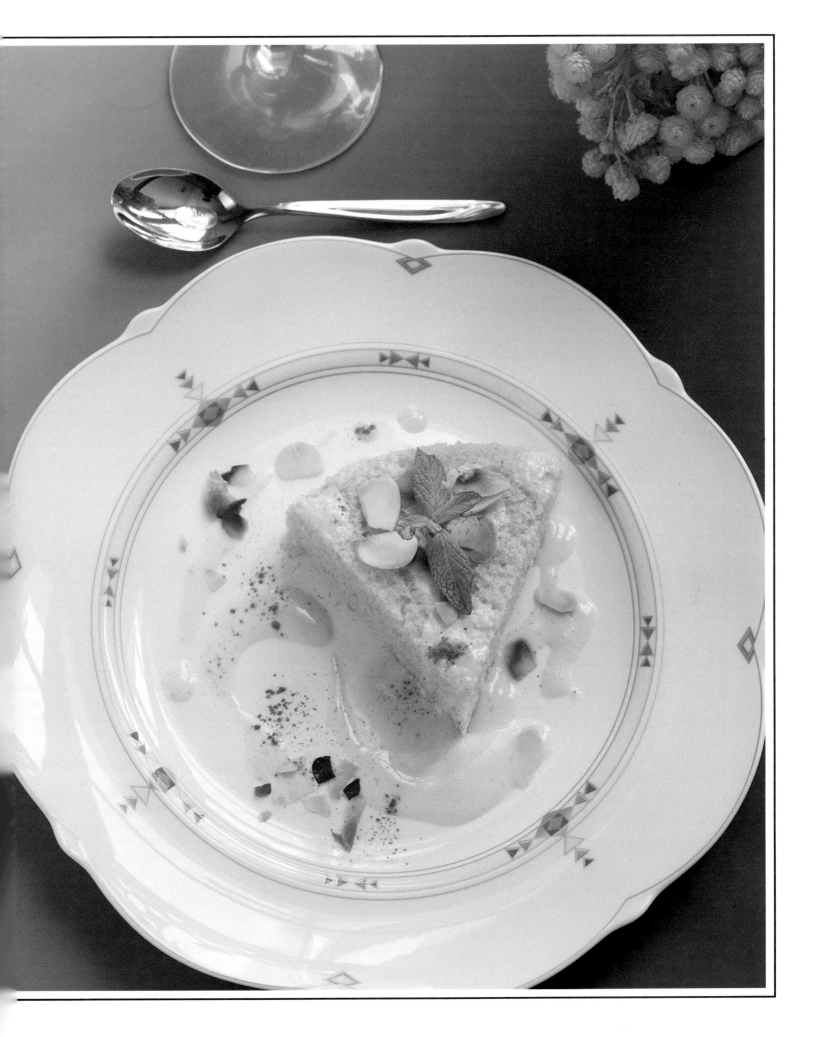

INGREDIENTS

- [ ] 125g/5oz butter at room temperature
- [ ] 65g/2¹/₂oz sugar
- [ ] 2 eggs
- [ ] 150g/6oz flour
- [ ] 1 tsp baking powder
- [ ] ¹/₂ tsp ground ginger
- [ ] 1 tsp mixed spice powder
- [ ] 6 egg yolks
- [ ] 75g/3oz sugar
- [ ] ¹/₂ litre/1 pint milk
- [ ] ¹/₂ tsp cinnamon
- [ ] 6 tbsps flaked almonds
- [ ] Small bunch fresh mint

1 In a bowl, beat 115g/4¹/₂oz butter until soft.

2 Add the sugar, beating the mixture well for 3 minutes.

3 In another bowl, beat the eggs. Whisk them gradually into the butter and sugar mixture.

4 Mix the baking powder, ginger and mixed spice into the flour. Add to the above and mix together well.

5

Grease a non-stick cake tin with the remaining butter, then pour in the cake mixture.

6

Cook the cake in a bain-marie in a moderate oven (180°C/350°F/Gas Mark 4) covered with a sheet of greaseproof paper, for 40 minutes.

7

Make the egg custard sauce by mixing together the egg yolks and sugar. Bring the milk to a boil.

8

Add the cinnamon to the egg yolk mixture, then pour over the milk. Whisk continuously, and pour back into the saucepan.

9

Cook over a very low heat, stirring constantly, until thickened (6 to 8 minutes). Remove from the heat.

10

Toast the flaked almonds under a hot grill, stirring as necessary until golden brown.

11

When the cake is done, (when an inserted blade comes out clean) turn out onto a cake rack to cool.

12

Cut into wedges, and serve with the cinnamon custard sauce, garnished with the flaked almonds and a few mint leaves.

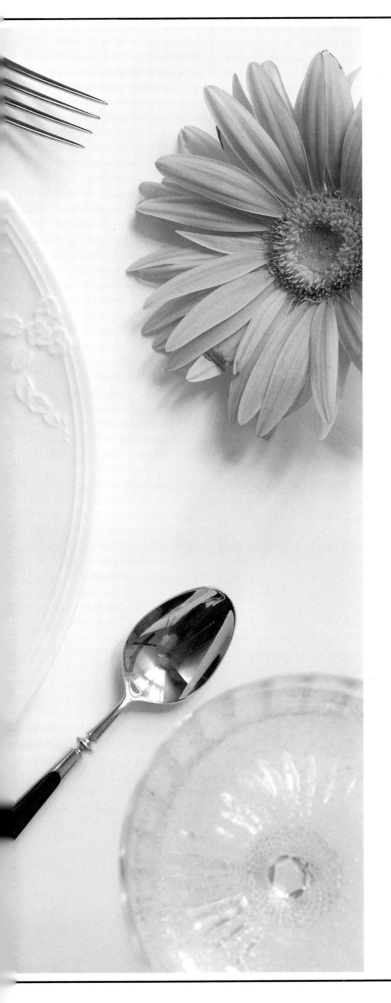

CRISP BANANA PASTRIES

WITH

CHOCOLATE SAUCE

SERVES : 6

PREPARATION TIME : 25 Minutes
COOKING TIME : 15 Minutes

*An original dessert sure to make an impression.
Little packets of filo pastry are filled with pastry
cream, sliced bananas and banana essence.
They are first browned in butter then baked and
served with a rich chocolate sauce.*

INGREDIENTS

- [ ] 2 egg yolks
- [ ] 50g/2oz sugar
- [ ] 25g/1oz flour
- [ ] ¼ litre/½ pint milk
- [ ] ½ tsp banana essence
- [ ] 4 bananas
- [ ] 6 sheets filo pastry
- [ ] 200g/8oz chocolate
- [ ] 5 tbsps double cream
- [ ] 4 tsps sugar
- [ ] 100ml/4 fl oz milk
- [ ] 40g/1½oz butter
- [ ] Few mint leaves
- [ ] 2 tbsps double cream

1 Make the pastry cream. In a bowl, mix together the egg yolks, sugar and the flour, until you obtain a thick, but smooth batter.

2 Bring the ¼ litre/½ pint milk to the boil and pour it over the egg yolk mixture, stirring rapidly. Pour this back into the saucepan.

3 Cook over a moderate heat, stirring constantly, until the mixture thickens as it comes to a boil. Stir in the banana essence, and allow to cool.

4 Peel the bananas and slice.

5 Spread 1 level tablespoon of sauce over the centre of each sheet of filo pastry.

6 Arrange the sliced banana over the cream, dividing the banana evenly between the six sheets.

7 Fold the filo sheets into pastries by bringing one side up and over the filling.

8 Fold over the other side of pastry, and press lightly.

9 Chop the chocolate, and place in a bowl with the cream, the 4 tsps sugar and the 100ml/4 fl oz milk. Melt over boiling water

10 Once the chocolate has melted, mix it gently with a whisk. Keep warm.Preheat the oven (200ºC/400ºF/Gas Mark 6).

11 In a large frying pan, melt the butter and fry the pastries for approximately 2 minutes each side. Transfer to a non-stick baking dish and bake in the preheated oven for 5 minutes.

12 Serve with the hot chocolate sauce and a little double cream, if desired.

FROZEN
KIWI MOUSSE
WITH
FRUIT PURÉE

SERVES : 6

PREPARATION TIME : 30 Minutes
COOKING TIME : 10 Minutes
SETTING TIME : 6 Hours

*A very attractive and colourful dessert, which
uses several different fruits. Individual mousses
of puréed kiwi and cream are set in the freezer.
They are served with a coulis of red fruit, either
strawberry or raspberry, and a lemon-flavoured
banana purée.*

INGREDIENTS

- [ ] 5 kiwi fruit
- [ ] 1½ packets powdered gelatine
- [ ] 350ml/14 fl oz treacle
- [ ] 300ml/12 fl oz double cream
- [ ] 200g/8oz strawberries
- [ ] 2 bananas
- [ ] ½ lemon
- [ ] Fresh mint

1 Peel the kiwi fruit, cut each into 4 lengthwise and remove the woody core.

2 Soak the gelatine in water. Press the kiwi fruit through a sieve, adding 1 tbsp water, or purée in a food processor.

3 In a saucepan, heat 150ml/6 fl oz of the treacle, and add the softened gelatine to the pan. Allow to cool and stir into the kiwi pulp. Mix well.

4 Place 200ml/6 fl oz of the cream in a bowl. Freeze for 5 minutes, then begin to whisk.

5

Whisk the cream gradually until thick and doubled in volume.

9

Mix with a hand-held mixer to obtain a liquid strawberry purée.

6

Using a spatula, fold the cream into the cooled kiwi mixture.

10

Strain the purée through a fine sieve to obtain a fine strawberry coulis.

7

Place 6 stainless steel rings or ramekins on a flat baking tray and ladle the mousse into them. Set in the freezer.

11

Peel the bananas. Cut into rounds. Add the remaining cream and treacle and juice from half a lemon. Blend until smooth to obtain a banana purée.

8

Bring 150ml/6 fl oz of the treacle to a boil and add the trimmed and washed strawberries. Remove from the heat and set aside for 5 minutes

12

Run a knife around the mousses to remove from the rings or ramekins. Unmould and serve with the strawberry coulis and banana purée. Decorate with the mint.

CREPES STUFFED

WITH

CHESTNUTS

SERVES : 6

PREPARATION TIME : 30 Minutes
COOKING TIME : 35 Minutes

This recipe uses canned chestnuts, which are available year-round. Classic crepes are filled with a pastry cream and the canned chestnuts and served cold with a raspberry, or other red fruit, purée.

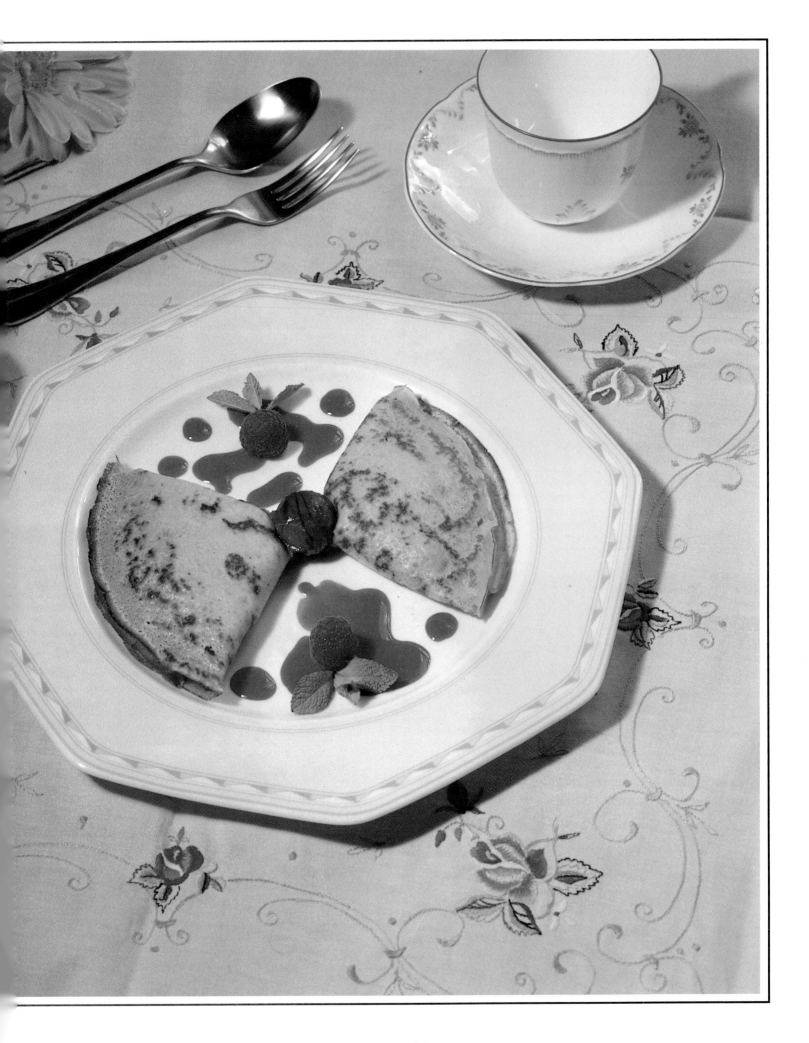

INGREDIENTS

- ☐ 200g/8oz flour
- ☐ 2 eggs
- ☐ 40g/1½oz sugar
- ☐ Pinch salt
- ☐ 400ml/14 fl oz milk
- ☐ 15g/½oz butter, melted
- ☐ 3 egg yolks
- ☐ 450g/1lb tin chestnuts in syrup
- ☐ 3 tbsps flour
- ☐ ¼ litre/½ pint milk
- ☐ 1 tbsp marasquin (or other flavoured liqueur)
- ☐ 150ml/6fl oz treacle
- ☐ 200g/8oz raspberries
- ☐ Oil
- ☐ Fresh mint

1 To make the crepe batter, beat together the flour, eggs, sugar and salt.

2 Add the 400ml/12 fl oz milk gradually, whisking continuously. Then whisk in the melted butter. Set aside to rest.

3 Make the pastry cream by whisking together the egg yolks with 4 tbsps of the chestnut syrup and 3 tbsps flour.

4 Bring the milk to a boil. Gradually whisk in the egg mixture. Mix together thoroughly and return to the pan to cook, stirring constantly.

5 When the mixture comes to a boil, remove from the heat and add the marasquin and 12 of the canned chestnuts, chopped.

6 Bring the treacle to a boil and add the raspberries. Set aside for 5 minutes.

7 Blend the treacle and raspberries to a smooth purée.

8 Strain the purée through a fine sieve to obtain a coulis.

9 Rub a frying pan with a sheet of kitchen paper dipped in oil before cooking each crepe. Add the batter to the pan using a small ladle.

10 Cook the first side for one minute, turn and cook the other side for a further minute. Repeat with the rest of the batter.

11 Spread each crepe with a little chestnut pastry cream. Fold into four to create small fans.

12 Serve the crepes hot with the raspberry coulis, a few whole canned chestnuts and bouquets of mint leaves.

PINEAPPLE

AND

MANGO

UPSIDE-DOWN CAKE

SERVES : 6

PREPARATION TIME : 30 to 35 Minutes
COOKING TIME : 50 Minutes

This is a variation on the classic pineapple upside-down cake. Chopped fresh or canned mango and rum are added to the batter. The cake is served with a purée of fresh raspberries.

INGREDIENTS

- ☐ 280g/11oz sugar
- ☐ 6 slices pineapple
- ☐ 1 mango
- ☐ 150g/6oz flour
- ☐ 2 tsps baking powder
- ☐ 5 eggs
- ☐ 100g/4oz butter
- ☐ 4 tbsps grated coconut
- ☐ 300ml/12 fl oz tinned pineapple juice
- ☐ 1 tbsp coconut liqueur
- ☐ 200g/8oz raspberry jam
- ☐ 3 tbsps double cream
- ☐ Few fresh mint leaves

1 Make a caramel by boiling together 100g/4oz of the sugar and 2 tbsps water in a non-stick frying pan.

2 When the caramel is golden brown, pour into the base of a cake tin.

3 Arrange the pineapple slices quickly over the hot caramel. Cool by dipping the base of the tin in cold water.

4 Halve the mango, remove the stone, then make crisscross slashes into the skin and flesh. Turn inside-out, and cut off the squares of flesh.